Response
and Recovery

By William T. Sanderson

Memiors of the World Trade Center Disaster

Above: The original cover. The buildings of the World Financial Center across the street from the World Trade Center, seen through a haze of smoke. Also victims of the terrorist attack, part of the collateral damage, their windows are broken and their rooftops lay shattered. Yet they survive, shining bright and standing tall in the sunlight.

Response and Recovery

Memoirs of the World Trade Center Disaster

By William Tiberius Sanderson

Published by

halfabook.com
http://www.halfabook.com

Copyright © 2001 by halfabook.com
Revised 2019

Dedicated to those who can keep the home fires burning, and put them out when they get out of control: Your hometown firemen.

Thank you for your support.

Manufactured in the United States of America

ISBN 9781588840219

Introduction

Response and Recovery is the terminology used by the Federal Emergency Management Agency to categorize two of the main phases of a disaster. The Agency's mission is to respond to a disaster and direct it towards recovery. On one level this book is about the event itself, the World Trade Center Disaster that occurred on September 11, 2001. On another level it is about an individual's response to that event and their subsequent recovery from dealing with the aftermath.

A lot has been said about the effects of Critical Incident Stress Syndrome and Post Traumatic Stress Disorder. The damage from September 11 ran deep, an entire city grieved and struggled with the aftermath. Not just a city, a nation grieved, moving forward towards a resolution of all the emotions experienced at the time. Anger, loss, sorrow, fear, anxiety, patriotism, empathy. Many of us run this gauntlet daily, just like the people in this book.

The events are real. Names have been changed and minor literary license has been taken in some places. This book is about the silent heroes, the paper pushers and the back office folks who work behind the scenes. They are not in the news, their jobs are not as glamorous as some, but they still have their role in history.

Please support your local fire and rescue. The equipment is expensive, the training dangerous and costly, and the sacrifice almost too much to ask. Public funds barely cover staffing and basic equipment like trucks and supplies. Many rely on volunteers who get little or no support, receive hand me downs, or are left to buy their own safety gear.

I have revised this book for new release. Enough time has passed from my employment with FEMA that I am no longer bound by job constraints. Also, despite the tragedy, 911 was an event that unified the country. Today, almost 20 years later, we are as divided as

Thank you for reading and sharing your thoughts. God Bless America. Keep us strong, Keep us safe. Pray for us.

William Tiberius Sanderson

PART I

RESPONSE

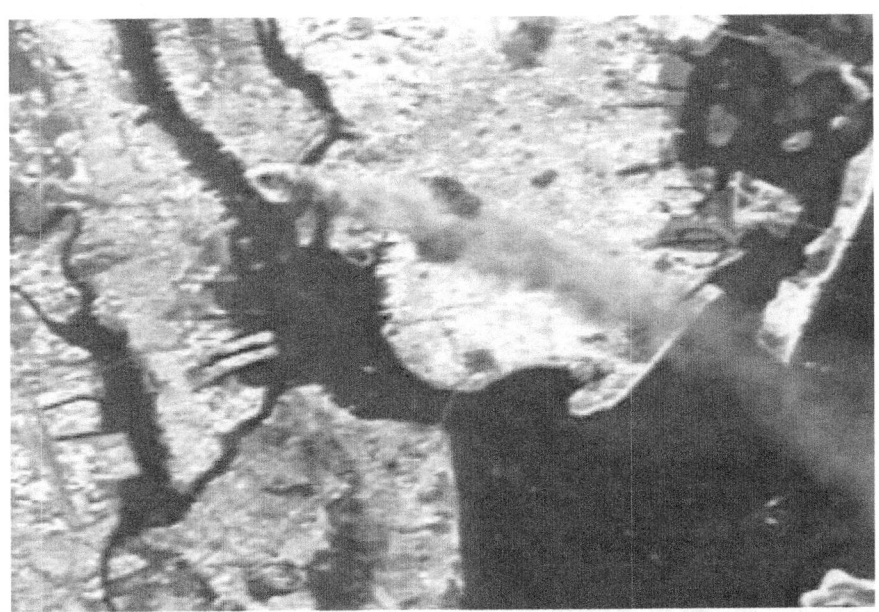

Smoke from the burning towers was visible from space as seen in this Internet photograph taken by a US astronaut.

Tuesday
September 11, 2001

Like most Americans, I get dressed and head off casually to work this morning. I am thinking about the new project I am on, tuning a network SQL server machine, a project that will task my abilities and challenge my skills. I am a computer consultant by trade, a contract worker with no home, moving in and out of companies that need my services. I have been reading and studying materials for days, preparing my approach while I work on a high level overview of what I intend to do to make the machine perform to expectations.

I enter the building, asking the receptionist to ring my supervisor. I am so new to the job that I have not been issued a security badge yet. While I wait the receptionist remarks about events she heard on the radio.

"The World Trade Center was hit by an airplane," she says. I immediately think it's an accident, a private plane off course that collided into the tower by mistake. My boss arrives and escorts me past two security doors, back to the cubicle where I am stationed. I don't mention the trade center. We talk briefly about my assignment and I prepare to get to work writing an overview of what I plan to do in the next few weeks to make the server faster.

I become aware of chatter from the cubicles around me. People are talking about the accident. A woman next to me has a radio on. She hears that the second tower has been hit and announces it to everyone within earshot. I begin to suspect what is now obvious. This is no accident.

In another cubicle a man is trying desperately to hit the major news sites on the Internet to verify the report. The sites are busy, as I imagine every office in the country is trying to do the same thing. He finally clicks on to CNN.com where a photo of the first tower in flames is graphically displayed. I glance over at it, a sick feeling churning in my gut. It is real. Since I am new on the job and a contractor I go back to my work, focusing on writing my report.

The woman in the next cube with the radio announces that a third plane has just hit the Pentagon. They think more attacks are coming. The office is now filled with alarm and conversation. Fear sweeps through the local community with announcements that the local mall will be closing. All plane flights have been canceled. Some people are sent home from downtown businesses. Then comes the news of a plane crash in Pennsylvania with suspicions that terrorists had something to do with that as well. My cell phone rings. It is my wife Bonnie asking me if I know anything of the events that have been occurring that morning. I am painfully aware, convinced beyond a shadow the doubt that this is no accident.

"You're going to go, aren't you?" she asks. It is the question I have been asking myself. After months without work, two days into a new contract I wonder myself if I am going to go. She already knows the answer, as do I. I am already thinking how I will break the news to my new employers that I am a reservist in the Federal Emergency Management Agency.

A few days before I had received an email from my cadre manager asking me if I would be available in February for service at the Olympics in Salt Lake City, Utah as part of FEMA's anti-terrorist group. I said yes immediately thinking that terrorism would never come this way, thinking that I would go to the Olympics where nothing would happen. How selfish that was! Now in the light of the events of the morning, again I come to the same conclusion. My country needs me. I will go.

I pick up the phone and dial the special number that tells FEMA that I am available and on call. The burning question has been answered. Now I must find a way to tell my employers.

The reports get worse. Sounds from the radio in the cubicle next to me are filled with panic. The world has changed forever. My coworkers are aghast. Their somber, sad faces that only hours ago could not imagine this terror now reflect the sentiments of a nation. I become firmer in my resolve.

I go over to my supervisor and tell him that I am a FEMA reservist and will probably be asked to come and support in the relief operation.

"What will you do?" he asks. "What kind of work do you do for FEMA?"

"I'm a specialist in Geographic Information Systems, GIS," I answer. "Usually I work hurricanes and floods. New York City is my home base, FEMA Region II, and it is likely I will have to go. I have no choice." He is curious so I continue. "I worked once in Rio Piedras in Puerto Rico where I mapped body removal and hazards after a building exploded from a gas leak. It is the only disaster I can remotely equate to this one. I imagine this work will be much the same."

I submit the paper outlining my plans for tuning the server. He reads it carefully. "This can wait," he finally says. "There is another job you have to do before you can finish this one. My question is, how long will you be gone?"

"Probably two weeks," I reply.

"Really?" he says in disbelief. "Only two weeks?" I can tell he doesn't believe me. I don't either, but he agrees that I must do what is necessary.

"I may not get the call," I tell him. "I'm telling you all this just in case." As the reports pour in from radios and web pages around me I somehow hope that I do not.

The rest of the day passes like a blur. My supervisor and I speak once again. I pack up and go home. The television is ablaze with coverage of the events of the day. No sooner then I settle in to watch, the phone rings. Bonnie answers and I hear her say, " Yes,

Louise we have been expecting your call." she passes the phone to me and immediately sets about doing what she has done so many times before. I hear her digging in the closet for my big green bag. I see her getting ready to do a load of laundry. She goes through the kitchen cabinets looking for snacks and munchies that keep me going.

Meanwhile I write down the phone number Louise has given me. All I know is that it is in Edison New Jersey. I argue that there are no planes flying so I get authorization to drive. I tell her thanks and I will see her tomorrow.

I call the number after I hang up but it is busy. The rest of the night is a flurry of activity. I compose several emails, a special one to my supervisor telling him that I got the call and will see him in two weeks. I tell him I will stop by in the morning to square things personally. Despite his approval and understanding, I am

worried about leaving him in a lurch. Bonnie goes to the grocery store where she stocks up on snacks that she will pack with my clothes. Meanwhile I go downstairs to my file cabinet where I gather the necessary materials that I will take to support my efforts. I have a library of data software and paperwork that I will need to do my job. "Be prepared," an old boy scout motto, is an understatement in the world of FEMA. Sometimes it can be days before supplies catch up with the response team. Friends joke when they say I parachute into a disaster with a laptop and a briefcase, but it is not far from the truth.

Rest comes uneasy that night. Bonnie and I talk after my son has gone to bed. I sense she is worried, but she knows I am doing the right thing.

After the collapse of the towers, smoke from the pile of debris burned for months.

Wednesday
September 12

The next morning I stop by the workplace on my way out of town. "I'll be back soon enough," I reassure my supervisor one more time. "I want to do the server job," I said. "I'll work twice as hard when I return."

"The work you have to do in New York is more important for the moment," he replies. He's very understanding. The look in his eye tells me he is sincere in his heart. He has strengthened my purpose.

"What are you going to be doing there again?" he asks, still curious. I show him a notebook that I have brought with me documenting some of the work that I did in Puerto Rico. The book contains maps of hazards in an exploded building with positions where bodies were removed, marked with little triangles.

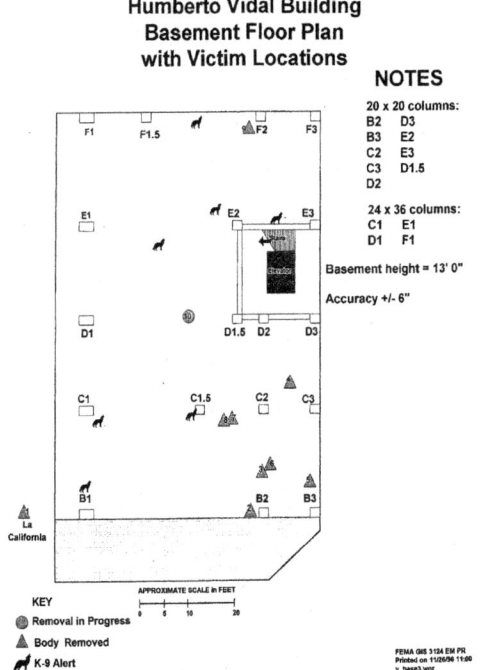

Humberto Vidal Building
Basement Floor Plan
with Victim Locations

NOTES

20 x 20 columns:
B2 D3
B3 E2
C2 E3
C3 D1.5
D2

24 x 36 columns:
C1 E1
D1 F1

Basement height = 13' 0"

Accuracy +/- 6"

KEY
Removal in Progress
Body Removed
K-9 Alert

APPROXIMATE SCALE in FEET

FEMA GIS 3124 EM PR
Printed on 11/26/96 11:00
v_base3.wor

Occasionally there is a figure of a little dog, showing the location of an alert where a dog detected something.

Something could be buried there and it tells the rescuers where to best focus their debris removal efforts. Each triangle has a number which is linked to a database of names, times, estimated age, and comments. Several of the names are Jane Doe.

I haven't looked at these maps in a while. When I made them it was the first time that I had

17

ever worked with Urban Search and Rescue or mapped something like this. I am used to hurricane paths, debris areas, generator locations, and critical points and facilities. I did the job at Rio Piedras, and did it well, but it was hard on me. Every now and then I would stop and realize what I was doing and get emotional for a minute, burying my face in the computer monitor so no one would notice. I hardly ever think about it anymore and I realize that I have put that experience well behind me.

I head out, assured by my supervisor again that I am doing the right thing. He is very patriotic. Some of my coworkers wish me well on the way out. I sense that most of them would like to come along and help. In times like these it is a natural reaction to want to reach out and help others. I tell them all I will do them and America proud. I feel like a soldier going off to war.

Once I am in my car and driving I begin this chronology, dictating the events and my thoughts into a small tape recorder. Eight hours pass on the road. Before long I find myself well beyond Pennsylvania and on the New Jersey Turnpike.

Finding a FEMA facility is always an interesting experience. They are often temporary locations and we never know what we will find or where it will be. One time it was a flight on a smoke jumper from a military base I reported to in Puerto Rico. Another time it was a cramped room in an old ammunition bunker where you had a choice of a table or a chair. Space was a premium at that disaster. The room stunk because the toilets  would not flush. They had run out of water after the hurricane had passed. Another time I arrived at a partially destroyed hotel that had been commandeered and surrounded with emergency vehicles, satellite trucks and US Marshals.

This time it is an old government facility in the middle of the New Jersey meadows.

I show my badge to the guard at the gate. He hands me a map, explaining the route I should take through what looks like an abandoned military base. The roads are overgrown with vegetation, the street signs rust with age and decay. Following the map I reach a white stucco warehouse brimming with activity. Telephone trucks line the front drive and men are busy digging lines and twisting wires. Up on the docks pallets of water are being loaded onto trucks. Generators and equipment are being staged and readied. I get directions to an office above the loading dock where several people point me to a pile of paperwork that I must fill out to properly check in. A woman is on the phone, a piece of paper in front of her filled with scribbles. I imagine she was the one I had just called from the turnpike asking directions. No sooner does she put the phone back on the cradle than it rings again. She takes a big gulp of water and answers it.

I turn in my completed paperwork and I am handed a map to another location. "This is where you're supposed to go."

I follow the map to a National Guard Armory. Security is tight. There are two tanks parked behind the gate and a truck blocks the entrance. The guards question me, scrutinizing my badge. They call inside to check. When I am cleared they apologize but I thank them for their diligence. I feel safe here.

The temporary FEMA office I will work in this time is normally a military training room in a low flat building on the base. I meet up with some old friends from other missions. We hug and look nervously at each other. This is not like anything we have encountered in the past. This is not a hurricane, a flood, an earthquake or even a tornado. This is a man made disaster. How do we handle this? That's okay, I am reminded. The "F" in FEMA stands for Flexible.

I set right to work, reading the Situation Report, a paper used to brief any newcomer on the status of the situation. I read that 30,000 body bags have been ordered and it is feared that this is not enough. There is mention of using 150 refrigerated trucks as morgues. I am shocked initially, but I remember what it was like to look at the number of commuters coming out of the subway system underneath the World Trade Center. I had stayed in the Marriott hotel that was located between the towers. I watched the people on their way to work in the morning, amazed at the sea of faces that worked inside those Towers.

From the Situation Report I glean the necessary information and began creating the standard FEMA maps required in every disaster. That is what I do, Geographical Information Systems Specialist, a fancy title for mapmaker. GIS is the marriage of technology and cartography. Points on a map are represented as data layers. In my go-kit I have data layers for most of the country, things such as county boundaries, rivers and lakes, streets, flood zone boundaries, city, state, and municipal boundaries, airports, churches, schools, even census data represented as block groups. I also have emergency data: locations of hospitals, military bases, police stations, fire stations, dams, and public buildings. By combining data layers and superimposing them I can create maps that tell things like the population in a given flood zone, locations of churches and schools that can serve as temporary shelters, and where the nearest military base can be found for hospital and airlift support.

For this disaster, designated DR-1391-NY, the President has declared all the surrounding counties of Manhattan are eligible for Individual Assistance and Public Assistance. I wonder why the area is so large. Why include Staten Island? Someone explains to me that the explosion was the equivalent of an earthquake measuring 2.6 on the Richter scale. There could be buildings and individuals miles away that have been affected. Many people across the river in New Jersey witnessed the destruction of the towers firsthand. I recall growing up in Jersey City watching the towers being built when I was a young boy. I create the declared map. I overhear from somewhere in the room that FEMA is looking for a location to set up the DFO, the Disaster Field Office. I began to put together another map showing the possible locations based on information provided by my superiors. Security seems to be a big issue on everyone's mind. Piers and docks, although included, seem to be unlikely candidates. "In event of an evacuation we'd have to jump out the windows," explains the Section Chief.

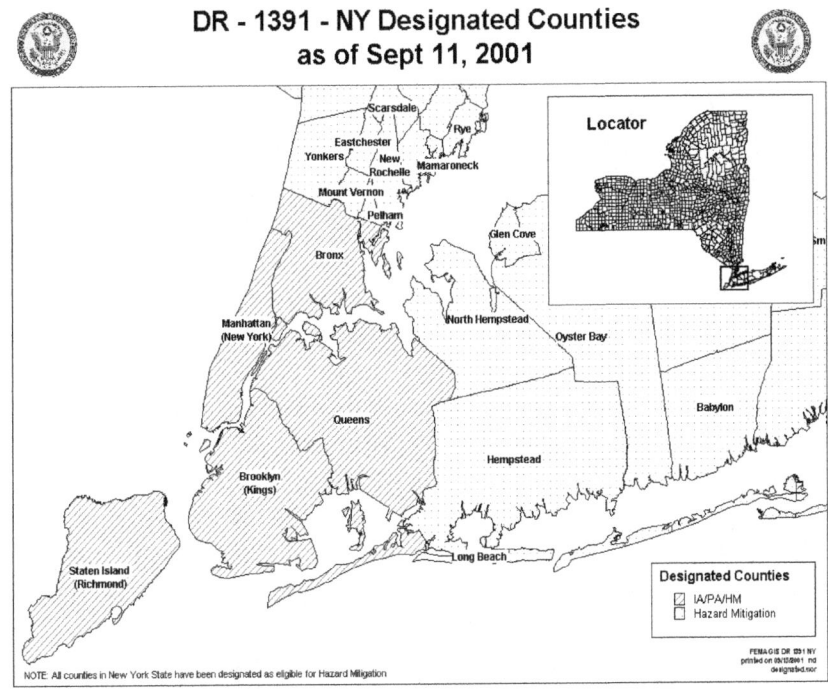

DR - 1391 - NY Designated Counties as of Sept 11, 2001

Louise, my cadre manager arrives. She thanks me for responding so quickly. It has been less than 24 hours since I received her call. I offer her some of the maps I have made. She explains to me some of the oddities I have encountered between the data in the computer and what I see on the tourist maps. Staten Island is really Kings County and the Bronx is Richmond. I find it odd that I grew up in this area and I never knew these things, but that is one reason I like GIS. Every time I go to a new location and create maps of that area I learn something new.

By the time I finish it is late. The night shift has arrived. We are in a twelve-hour operational period, which means all the reports and briefings must be updated and published every twelve hours. They will include my maps in the next briefing. I'm free to leave.

I have a hotel reservation an hour or more away. I feel lost as I weave between the tanks on my way off the base. Most of the cars are turning left which I figure leads to the interstate or the Turnpike. I follow them blindly, a lemming unsure of where I am going. I am still thinking about the Towers, about seeing them built. I think about the New York blackout, the last disaster I saw from the Jersey shores. I try to imagine what this will look like. I really didn't get to see much of the television coverage before I had to leave.

I am lost. All the cars have turned in other directions somewhere up the road. Something however looks familiar. I think I am near my brother's house. I remember Bonnie telling me I would be near him. His number is programmed into my cell phone so I give him a call. It turns out that I am less than five minutes away. He gives me directions and I look forward to spending time with family instead of alone in a hotel room. That is not where I want to be tonight, even though I usually spend the first night of any deployment alone in a hotel room.

My brother welcomes me warmly. We sit down in front of his big screen television and talk far into the night, discussing current events and our reactions. I finally get to see some television, the scenes that have been replayed over and over in living rooms across America. It runs like a Hollywood movie on the big screen, like an endless loop over and over. I praise the special effects wizards in the industry, amazed at how life like the disaster movies have been. I remind myself this is real, and art has imitated life, or is it vice versa.

"This city has a strong ethnic population," my brother tells me, speaking of the town where he lives. "I usually get gas at a local station owned by an Arabic guy. This morning there were no lines there. Cars were passing by the Cars were passing by the

22

local business owned by dark skin Iraqi immigrants in favor of the American looking Texaco station."

"Trust your car to the man with the star," I say. America has entered a new age of racism.

"You know some kids at a local high school were protesting, yelling things like *Down with America*, and *Death to the Infidels*," says my sister-in-law. "They were celebrating the destruction of the Towers."

"Why live in this country if that's how you feel?" asks my brother. "If it's so bad here why not go back to your homeland?"

Me? I like America. I am a third generation Italian. My grandparents paid their dues at Ellis Island. I grew up in a ghetto. My dad worked his way out of there, running a printing business with my uncle out of the basement of the tenement we lived in. That was at night, he had a day job as well. This is the land of opportunity. I believe in everyone having a shot at the American Dream. Following my father's example, I have also worked hard so my family can share in the good life. I am even beginning to sound like my father, but where else but in America can you do this?

I have seen the ugly side of prejudice, too. I have seen discrimination and reverse discrimination. This is a difficult situation when the enemy is among us. Are these kids protesting innocently or are they really immersed in what they consider is a just cause? Prejudice knows no boundary and often hate is misdirected at the wrong individual. I don't feel hatred right now, only the sense of loss.

I am fearful and tired and I go to bed in the family guest room, grateful that it is not another lonely hotel room.

Smoke rises over South Manhatten, as seen from across the Hudson River in New Jersey.

Thursday
September 13

The alarm rings at 5 am. My sister in law has done a wonderful thing. She has timed the coffee maker to perk when I wake up and has placed a to-go cup next to it along with a note. There is a bag of snacks packed and ready for me to take to work. I head off to the military compound again. I get the same security treatment at the gate. The guards scrutinize everything and even check the trunk this time. Once again I am happy for their diligence, and I report this to Bonnie the next time I talk to her.

Inside I pick up the latest Situation Report and read the statistics again. New information on the report is always italicized. The first thing I notice is that the number of people reported missing has gone up. There is also a growing count of how many bodies have been removed to date. I set to work updating and printing out a few more maps. Then I wait to see what's going on like everyone else. I wonder why we are in New Jersey so far away from the incident itself. I remind myself that security is a major concern

The phone keeps ringing and I keep answering it. Most of the time I am conveying information. There is a list of current phone numbers on the blackboard. One call comes in from the weather service. They are concerned and tracking weather in the area for us. Rain seems to generate the most concern. If it rains, the concrete will react with the water and solidify, making it more difficult to dig out the rubble. I post the weather report on the bulletin board and make a copy for the files per standard operating procedures. It will go into the next round of reports that are produced every 12 hours by the Information and Planning section.

A man from Operations comes in. "I need a map of the two block radius around the World Trade Center." He sounds desperate and there is something in his voice. "I need to see the buildings on the map, or more properly, where they once were."

"I don't have building footprint data, but I have a tourist map," I say. "I can draw them in, but they may not be that accurate."

"I don't care," he replies. "There are no buildings there anymore, just a vague idea of where they once were."

I start working on the map and he comes back in a little while. "Can you make it a four block radius around the World Trade Center?" he asks. I get the impression that the size of the event has grown. "Also, can you change the colors of the buildings that have collapsed to make them stand out on the map?"

That is something easy to do in GIS. I start by creating a table of collapsed buildings with a status column to run a theme and shade them to his specifications. Before I finish the map he returns again. "There was a hotel located between the towers that has also partially collapsed," he says.

I have already drawn it in. I change the colors accordingly and print out the maps. "Who are these maps are for?" I ask

"For the teams working at the World Trade Center right now," he replies.

"You're going to need a courier to deliver them," I say. There is no courier of course.

"What I really need is GIS located closer to the incident," he says. I can see by the look in his eyes that he is desperate to do something to help the people working at the site. I ask my section chief for permission to go forward and support them, whoever they are. He gives me the go, knowing that he has enough maps for now and that another GIS tech has been deployed and will be reporting in later for the night shift.

I pack up my laptop, grab the snacks and head off. I have a name and a location, nothing more. I have a vague idea of where the New Jersey Turnpike is from here. I have a handful of printed maps, but I am excited with a strong sense of purpose.

At the gate there is a man wearing a FEMA badge standing next to a suitcase. He is waiting for a taxicab.

"Where are you going?" I ask him.

"Probably the same place you are," he replies. I recognize him from Texas where we worked a flood disaster together. "I know the New York area well," he says. "I have an apartment in Manhattan, and I'm willing to help navigate to our destination."

"Hop in," I say, popping the trunk for his luggage.

We talk while driving. He tells me that he was at a black tie affair the night before when he got the word to report. Like me, he thinks all of the action is in the city, not at a military base 50 or 60 miles away. He is a Harvard graduate, a management consultant who works for the Public Information Section as a FEMA reservist. So many of us have other jobs. Thank God. I would not want to make a full time living off disasters. He loves his job and he knows how important it will be to disseminate the right information to the news media. He knows he will be talking to major networks on this one. He takes his job serious.

As we near the city I see a plume of smoke where the towers once where. The traffic is congested on the Turnpike; the Holland Tunnel is closed to all but emergency vehicles. We have joined a stream of traffic heading north toward the Lincoln tunnel, one of the few arteries into the city. My navigator says to avoid the first exit for the tunnel, hoping the second will be less congested. He guesses right. As we turn off the expressway towards the tunnel, the view from the ramp of a smoldering south Manhattan silences us both.

The traffic is a nightmare once we come out of the tunnel. We move forward one foot at the time, crawling in a city that has been paralyzed. My navigator wants desperately to stop by his apartment before we report in. He has no clothes to wear other than what he has been wearing for two days so I agree to take him there.

The police are everywhere directing traffic but it is still congested and we stop often. We finally reach his neighborhood. I wait on the street in a loading zone while he runs up to his apartment. I pass the time looking at the faces of the New Yorkers as they walk down the street. Some show panic, some show fear, some I imagine look the same as they always do. I see people going about trying to do normal things. A mother is escorting a daughter in a school uniform; some students are walking together carrying books over their shoulders, a kid on roller blades scoots by. A small group of people sits on a nearby porch smoking cigarettes and drinking coffee.

The navigator is back now wearing a fresh FEMA shirt. We pull out into the stream of endless traffic, cars and trucks trying to make their way slowly toward their destinations. I'm always confused about the one-way streets in New York and I'm glad he is with me to tell me where to turn. He knows exactly where we are going.

We are headed to the Jacob Javits Convention Center. As we approach the area there are police everywhere. The streets are barricaded within a block of our destination but after showing our badges we are allowed to pass. I drive around the building, a huge convention hall, looking for a parking place. All I know is that somewhere inside this massive building there is a FEMA office. We park around the corner on the street. This building is also the location where volunteers have flocked to lend aid to the disaster. The mob of people surges in a confused and angry sea. We pass a line that goes around the block along the side wall of the building. Some people have blankets and are on the ground sleeping. It is the type of line you'd expect to see at a rock concert or the opening of first run movie. I have seen Star Wars fans camped out in a similar fashion.

Remnants of a former trade show, hastily disbanded, litter the floor of the convention center.

I see another reason for the line. Further along the Salvation Army and the Red Cross have set up mobile feeding units dispensing meals to these these tired people. We finally find the entrance, a crowded corridor guarded by two policemen. We again show our badges and we are told that the FEMA offices are on the other side of the building. We set off to find it, a task that quickly becomes a challenge. Someone tells us that we have to go through the building and outside to a loading dock, then back in another hall and up a ramp to find where we need to report. This place is huge. We pass through one large hall where a trade show is hastily being broken down to make room for something new. A man moving pallets around with a forklift stops to ask me how long we will be there, meaning FEMA, since we are both wearing FEMA shirts. I tell him I don't know, maybe a month. He says "I hope so, I can't make any money with you guys here. I'm used to doing 2 or 3 of these trade shows a week." He is referring to his job of breaking down and assembling booths and kiosks for the constant turnover of new trade shows and conventions. You could easily run that many shows out of this massive building.

It is the first time I have heard of FEMA putting someone out of work. I know it is just his fears. In reality there will be plenty of work for him to do in the coming weeks.

We continue to follow the directions we have and finally enter a huge hall. It would normally be set up for conventions or trade shows, but now it is a thriving FEMA command center. There are military guards posted around the entrance. They check our IDs carefully. We pass through the checkpoint. The hall is filled with smaller areas cordoned off with curtains. I recognize the earmarks of ESF-9, Urban Search and Rescue. These guys do not stay in fancy hotels, they eat when they can, and they sleep where they can. Behind the curtains I see tents and an occasional recreational vehicle. There are cots and blankets and pillows. Outside each area, a sign hangs proudly telling me who is billeted in this area. There are units from Puerto Rico, Massachusetts, Sacramento, Riverside, Miami, Missouri, Indiana, Ohio, Louisiana, Pennsylvania and New Jersey. I've never seen so many Urban Search and Rescue units in one place. I am gaping like a tourist, like anyone would around all this activity. I see MERS units, Mobile Emergency Response Specialists, set up in the corner with a van that is a mobile office containing computers and communication equipment. I pass a bank of telephones where off duty rescue personnel sit in casual attire while talking to their loved ones.

I pass through one set of curtains into the Incident Command Post area. I see an old friend, one I hadn't seen since Rio Piedras. He was the man who gave me a search and rescue patch at the end of that operation. It really made me feel like I was part of the team. He thought the maps that I made during that operation were useful tools and very needed. He is glad to see me. He has already told the rest of the team about what I had done there and built their expectations about how good I was. "If only you were here," he says to me, repeating what he has been saying all morning. I finally feel like I am finally in the right place, a place where I can do some good.

I report to a guy named Brutus, head of Information and Planning for ESF-9, the FEMA acronym for Urban Search and Rescue. He also makes me feel welcome and is glad to see that I brought some maps with me. " I requested those" he says, looking them over. "Good. You also made maps of the four-block area around the World Trade Center. This mess gets bigger by the moment." He takes a couple of the maps and puts them on the table where people can get them, then he points to a location where I can set up shop.

I squeeze myself around a table next to a New Jersey State Trooper who has also come to help. He answers the phone a lot and gives out useful information. After talking to him between calls I learn that he expected to do more than just answer phones. He is used to more action in a situation like this. His main function at his normal job is to respond to hazardous spills and emergency situations dealing with public safety. I didn't tell him at the time how really useful he was just getting people in touch with each other and directing them to the right groups. It is just as important a job as bringing order to the rubble and sorting out the chaos at the scene of the disaster. Every connection he makes helps the relief effort become more organized in these early days. It is a critical task, but he is unaware of it and complains about being stuck with this job.

The maps I have brought with me disappear quickly, I must print more. I borrow a printer cable, nudge someone off their printer, and squeeze out a better copy. A high-speed copier has been set up in this area. I am always amazed at how these FEMA offices manage to quickly get the essential conveniences of any modern office.

I have spoken too soon. I meet Greg, the man who is to become my boss. He tells me that he has been crying for resources all morning. He can't even get a pencil, but he's glad to see me. He says he's been requesting me ever since he got there. He's also looking for something called an Adobe projector and he tells me there is a deployable GIS suite en-route with plotters and printers and workstations. I won't be on the laptop forever.

He looks at the maps I have made and has me update them again. A portion of the buildings designated as World Trade Center 4 and 5 have collapsed. These are the buildings on the west side of the plaza, the L-shaped ones that contain stores like Borders Books and the coffee shop. I publish the new maps, changing the colors because all I have are black-and-white printers for the moment. I think of how nice it will be to have all the GIS equipment that I normally have at my disposal, but small 8 1/2 by eleven black and white maps will have to do.

I work hard at my job but sometimes I am distracted or drawn into other business. Greg would prefer that I sit isolated in the corner producing maps in some imagined haven of quiet. I have seen that only a few times in my career with FEMA, and only when GIS is located in a private room hidden somewhere in the disaster field office where no one can find it. Creating maps is a tedious process and at times I welcome the distraction. Someone is telling me that a school of acupuncture and massage is ready to set up and give free massages to all the relief workers. All they need is a letter authorizing them. I get the information and pass it along to the right person, smiling later when I see them setting up in a quiet area overlooking the convention hall. I wonder if that room would not have been a good location for GIS.

It is late, almost 1:00 AM, I hastily make a reservation at a nearby hotel, feeling lucky to get a room. Later I learned that there were plenty of rooms. New York tourism is at an all-time low despite the fact that September is off-season.

I pack up the computer and gather the rest of my gear. I travel with an extra bag of go kit materials which burdens me down, things like blank GIS request forms and paperwork, a book of phone numbers and contacts I have accumulated over the years, a list of private and public FTP sites that are sources of relevant information, and a wallet full of CDs containing data and programs that I will need to do my job. I even bought a ream of paper in case there was none available. Sorry Greg, I did not bring pencils, only pens. Another item I will add that to my list for the next time.

Friday
September 14

6:00 AM comes pretty early but I know that coffee and adrenaline will keep me going once I get to the office. The hotel, a luxurious facility located at Times Square, provides in-room coffee pots but they make you buy the coffee from the mini bar. This used to be free but they have changed their policy since the last time I have stayed here. Parking is $45 per day for guests, and I read in the guest directory that there is a $20 corkage charge per bottle if you bring your own liquor into the room. I have concierge privileges but I am always at work when the lounge is open. Most of the hotels in this chain provide these services for free, and I am used to it. Government workers at my level are not wealthy and usually squeeze every penny out of their paycheck. I am complaining because I am dying for a cup of coffee first thing in the morning. I must remember to add some coffee to the list of snacks and supplies that Bonnie packs for me.

Greg is staying in the same hotel so we ride to work together. Near the convention center I once again park far away, telling myself I must find a closer parking place. The laptop and bag of supplies weigh heavily on my shoulders. Greg complains as well. As we approach our work area he passes me instructions, telling me to check on that GIS equipment first thing. It is supposed to be on its way, he says. I sense he is losing faith with the system. I can only imagine what the logistics are to mobilize an operation of this size, especially when all the planes are grounded and traffic in the city is at a near standstill.

I update the maps again. Another building has partially collapsed overnight. The search and rescue teams point out other discrepancies in my maps. There is a collapsed bridge on the northwest side of the Trade Center and another one south of there that remains intact. There was a small orthodox church across the street and south of the World Trade Center. It also collapsed. One rescue worker seems adamant about getting it correctly located on the map, almost obsessed. After a while I tend to agree with him.

The destruction of the house of God does no one honor, and the tiny square on the map that represents the fallen church becomes a small tombstone in my mind.

The GIS equipment is still not here. Everyone says it is coming. Greg is not optimistic. He tells me a long story about why the space shuttle exploded. In short, pressure was put upon NASA to launch the shuttle on Friday instead of Saturday. There was a teacher on board this particular flight who was supposed to teach her classroom from space. If the shuttle launched on Saturday, there would be no audience for the class. One man on the launch team refused to vote in favor of launching the shuttle on Friday. He wanted to perform extra safety checks. The rest of the team pressured him and, against his better judgment, he voted in favor of the launch on Friday. The rest is history. The shuttle exploded.

The point Greg is trying to make involves trusting the system. He warns me that I have far too much trust in the system. He ends this conversation by once again complaining about not having any pencils.

I call FEMA headquarters in Washington and they tell me that the system is on the way. That's good enough for me; I have other things to do. Word is that the President is coming for a visit today. Nobody seems to know when or what time but he's definitely coming. Maybe he'll be here with the Deployable GIS Suite, I joke. The walls are bare. There are no displays or large maps arranged on them. Greg says we need to dress the place up a bit for the President. I am wondering what to do.

As if in answer, a man from a local Kinkos* introduces himself to me and offers his help. Not only his help but also the full resources of his store. He is a Commercial Account Manager. I tell him my problems and he tells me they have scanners and large plotters that can take my small maps and scale them up. I tell Greg we have a way of getting the job done and prettying up the place for the Presidential visit. I pack up my laptop grab some of the small maps that are lying around and proceed to follow this man five blocks away to a Kinkos store.

He is very proud of his store. It is brand-new and has just opened up. Then he tells me that he was at the Kinkos two blocks away from the World Trade Center when it exploded. None of the employees were hurt and he tells me that I will meet some of them at the store. He is making sure that they all have work. I get the sense that his willingness to help has something personal in it. At the store everyone is impressed with our arrival. I am wearing a FEMA shirt and I remember at one time how the appearance of FEMA calmed me in a troubled time. After losing everything following a hurricane in Saint Thomas, with looting the order of the day, and rapes and thefts in our neighborhood, FEMA was a godsend. I know how they feel. I am proud to wear this uniform

---

*   Kinkos is the former name of FedEx Kinkos, now simply FedEx Office, a store that supplies business support through a variety of products.

and I am always conscious of the special duty involved with wearing it.

One of the mandates I learned was to listen to people when they talk about their disaster experiences. Following a life threatening situation people want to talk about what they went through. I wanted to tell my story to the world. I had survived death by hurricane and talking about it was an affirmation of life. Listening has paid off. You wouldn't believe some of the stories I have heard. The power of human compassion and the superhuman abilities that come out in such times, it gives me faith in our species. It is funny how quickly we can forget our differences and how easily we can join together for a common cause under such duress. Like fine metals purified in the hottest fires, God tests us through adversity by giving us the opportunity to forge our spirit.

And, oh yes, there is human slag that surfaces as well.

The store is a busy place. There is a public area to the side with computers that can be rented. Several people are there making signs with pictures of their loved ones on them. One person has ordered many copies. Later I see these signs posted everywhere in town, especially near ground zero.

The Account Manager assigns people to help me. "Give him anything he needs," he tells a subordinate.

I pull out the maps that I have brought with me. "Can you enlarge these into wall displays?" I ask.

"Yes," he replies. He takes the maps and quickly disappears, returning after a moment. "Would you like them laminated?" he asks.

"Not necessary," I reply.

"What kind of paper?" he asks.

I look at the plotter they are going to print on. It is loaded with standard bright inkjet paper. "That will do," I say.

"Is there anything else we can do?"

I show him a small picture that I have of the World Trade Center before the disaster. "Can you scan it and enlarge it for me?" I ask.

"No problem. How many copies?"

It will take some time. I set up my laptop in one of the booths near the back and begin updating the latest base of operations map. I left in such a hurry that I did not have time to make the changes for the daily briefing. The Area Sales Manager comes over and sees what I am doing.

"There was an excellent map of the downtown area in the New York Times this morning," he says. He has a copy of the paper and shows it to me. It is almost exactly what I'm trying to depict on my maps. The buildings are labeled, they are colored according to their status, collapsed, intact, burning, partially collapsed.

"Maybe we can scan it," he suggests. Then he has a better idea. "Why don't I go to the Times and just get it." Before I can think it over he makes a quick phone call and is off. I go back to updating my maps, saving them as image files, and giving them to the Kinkos team to print out.

Someone else from the FEMA office shows up. They have a bundle of small signs and materials that they need blown up and laminated. One of them is a forest service ranger, normally used to fire fighting disasters. One thing I have noticed about these forest service people: they are willing to do anything to help and they do it with a smile. A policeman has escorted him here.

"If we're not back at the field office by 3:00, we won't be allowed in the building for security reasons," the ranger tells me.

"I have to get back before then to post all of the images and copies that I have," I explain. "Do you think I could catch a ride with you?" I ask.

The ranger looks at the policeman. "I don't know," he says. "The back seat is full of luggage and there's no room."

"I'm willing to squeeze in," I say.

"I'm not sure," he explains. "It's really full. We have no room because we have all this luggage with us. We haven't unloaded it yet."

"Thanks," I say politely.

He must feel the dejection. Once again the human desire to help someone overrides the first response. "Let me see if I can make some room. I might be able to get some of it in the trunk at least."

"I don't mind being cramped," I say. It is preferable to walking back with all the maps and my laptop in tow.

The Account Manager returns with a CD from the New York Times containing the image from the paper. He has a receipt for $0.00. "They are honored to help as long as we give them credit," he says. He makes 100 small copies and sends two to the big plotter.

An accident occurs on the corner and the traffic is horrible outside. I see why there is no room in the police car. The back is full of luggage and there are two policemen in the car as well. I wondered where they fit the forest ranger. Having witnessed the accident they do what all policemen do, they jump out of the car and begin to direct traffic and tend to the injured. It is 2:30 and I wonder if I will make it back on time to prepare for the Presidential visit.

Time seems to pass slowly and before long is 3:30. The New York Police have arrived and are taking control of the accident scene. One of our policemen comes inside saying we have to go. We grab all the materials that are done. The Account Manager promises to bring the rest to us when they are finished. We tell him to call first knowing that no one will be allowed in the building once the President is on-site. I leave, finding the back seat of the police cruiser spotless. The forest service guy is amazed. "Where did you put it all?" he asks.

"We found room in the trunk," he replies.

" Can we hurry?" I ask. "Or they won't let us back in the building."

"Don't worry," says the policemen driving. " You're with us. We *are* the security." he turns on his lights, whoops the siren a few times, and the New York Police directing traffic clear a path for him. The trip takes no time at all and turns out to be fun. Security is now even tighter at the convention center. There are helicopters circling overhead. The road out front is blocked off. They drop us off at the front door and we scurry to the next security post. The guard tells us it's OK, they have taken the President to Ground Zero first. I have plenty of time. They say it will be more like 5:00 before he arrives.

I post the big maps, the pictures, and the New York Times map on temporary plywood walls around the briefing area. The large aerial image of the World Trade Center before the disaster draws an immediate audience. As I put up the other displays I hear the search and rescue men pointing at objects in the picture as they talk. The picture shows the large golden ball that was the centerpiece of the fountain. "Amazing that survived," comments one of them.

There is a corrugated metal door that closes off the convention center. I hear it being lowered as we are locked down for the visit. We are all told to secure our areas and muster in the main aisle where the President will come. We are briefed on what to expect. The President will walk down one side of the aisle and talk to everyone on his left and then turn around and follow the opposite line back out the way he came so that everyone gets a chance to meet him. I was late getting to the assembly and I find myself standing on a chair in the back of the crowd hoping to catch a glimpse of him.

People in the front are excited. I look down the crowded aisle and see a bright bank of lights that usually follow every dignitary, the ever present media. The lights are moving slow, the President is taking time to meet everyone as was promised. He poses for pictures with many of the search and rescue people. Someone hands him a red Army Corps of Engineers baseball cap.

He puts it on with a silly grin while a bunch of red shirts gather around him to have their picture taken.

The mayor of New York, Mayor Rudy Giuliani, has led the way shaking hands with everyone and thanking us for our heroic efforts. I reach my hand out and he clasps it firmly. He thanks us for coming to New York to help the city in its hour of need. Firemen and people in the front are awestruck by his presence.

Hillary Clinton has already come and gone, disappearing out the back, never coming all the way to the front where I am waiting. I am still standing on a chair looking down the ranks. The bright lights have also left. They are no longer following the President. He is getting closer.

A man is also standing on a chair next to me. He tells me he is from a government brain trust somewhere in Maryland. In his hand he is holding a flashlight that has been modified to become a radar that can sense movement in a debris pile. I had met him earlier in the day. Two teams had arrived with similar devices that could probe the debris for survivors. Both wanted to lend their help but suffered from a similar problem. The devices would only work in complete silence. With all the debris removal and searching going on at the disaster site they may never have the chance to test their devices.

I had told him to be patient, not to lose hope, and that an opportunity would present itself if he waited for the right moment. It eventually did and he had his moment of fame. His spirit reflected a similar hope that was with everyone who came to New York to help. They came ready and eager and were told to be patient, and this was only the beginning, the early days of the massive relief effort that would be mounted. The first that arrived were welcomed with open arms, but later I would see the tide of support threaten to overwhelm the rescue effort and sink it in a sea of confusion.

The man is holding his flashlight device in his hand. He passes the time waiting and tells me that this was just a little side

project. His team's whole job is to sit around and think up new ideas and new applications of technology. The main research for this particular radar product had something to do with missiles. I can see how proud he is of it, a way of applying the technology for life rather than death.

The President comes by and I shake his hand. He answers all our questions. He tells us to pray because he has been praying a lot. He thanks us for doing this difficult job. Then his expression changes for a moment and he gets that look, the look of anyone who has visited Ground Zero. I have seen it in many of the faces of the search and rescue teams, and in my own face in the mirror.

I snap several pictures. The man next to me with the flashlight device offers to takes my picture with the President. We work our way around to the end of the line where I have my opportunity. My own patience pays off and I don't think there was anyone after me. I walk up to him and he puts his arm around me like I'm an old friend. The President! "Thanks for you help," he says to me.

"Thank you, Mr. President," I say.

"No, thank you," he says. "Work hard."

"I know you are," I say. "I'll pray for you and our country." He smiles and my friend snaps the picture.

Greg was next to me. He begins talking very matter of factly to the President. I almost think he is going to complain about not having any pencils. But he has his peace, venting to the Commander-in-Chief. The President listens patiently. He smiles and waves, then turns and leaves, escorted by secret servicemen that I hadn't even noticed before.

We all go back to work with renewed strength. The visit has been very helpful and great for morale. Personally I can't believe I have met the President. Even Greg seems happier now, except that he reminds me that we still have no GIS equipment. And he still has no pencils.

Saturday
September 15

Greg is suiting up to go down to Ground Zero. A man
named Stavros shows up, a tall blond battalion chief and fire
department veteran. He recognizes Greg and they both embrace.
He asks what he can do to help. Greg tells him to check in. He has
come without authorization. He was in training in New Jersey
traveling on his way back to California when he heard about the
disaster. He called his wife and told her that he was heading in the
wrong direction. She urged him to turn around and go back to the
city.

He does not have his search and rescue gear with him but
somehow they find him everything he needs. Greg calls him Jethro
because he has borrowed a pair of pants from somebody that is two
sizes too big. To keep them up he has tied the loops together with a
piece of rope. As they get ready to leave, Greg harasses me one
more time about the GIS equipment not being here.

"It will be here," I assure him.

"Right!" he says sarcastically.

"It's arriving today," I say. "I have been assured by
Washington."

He blasts Washington. "They can't even get me a friggin
pencil!"

"It's on the way," I say with conviction.

"Wanna bet on it?"

"Name your price."

"A pitcher of beer at an Irish pub."

"You're on!" We shake on it.

Greg laughs, confident it's a sure thing. He finalizes it by
saying, "If it's not here by 3:00 you owe me, buddy."

He's gone about an hour when I get a call from my wife Bonnie. "You're equipment is there, honey," she says.

"What equipment?" I ask.

"They just called me here at the house. Your equipment is there. You're at a convention center, right?"

"Yeah," I reply, dumbstruck.

"Your GIS equipment. It's there! I have a phone number of a woman who has been trying to get in contact with you."

This is just another one of those situations where a man's wife knows more than he does. I laugh. She is in the loop and I'm not. All I can say is, "I love you honey."

"I know," she replies in her best Princess Leia imitation.

I get off the phone with her and call Washington to verify this. They tell me the equipment was sent by truck from the FEMA Center at Mt. Weather, Virginia the night before. It should be there already. I no sooner get off the phone with them when it rings again.

A woman is asking for me. "I'm with forest service logistics," she says. "I've been trying to contact you to accept delivery of this equipment." Using my cell phone and her instructions, I navigate my way through the vast hall to where she is. She is glad to see me and it is obvious that one of her priorities has been to get this equipment to its final destination. I am anxious to see it. She takes me outside and across the street to a dingy warehouse. The floor is thick with dirt and dust, as if it has not been used for years. It is an old brick building, looking like it may collapse at any moment. We climb up onto the loading dock. There are no ladders and we help lift each other up. There I recognize the familiar transit cases, large red fiberglass boxes on wheels. It is the red suite, a system I had just packed up in Texas less than a month ago. Each box is marked one of thirteen, two of thirteen, three of thirteen, etc. The logistics lady checks them off on a bill of laden as we verify and see that they are all here.

"You can open them here and inventory the contents, or wait until they get unpacked at their final destination," she says.

"You bring them next door and I'll unpack them. All you will have to do is inventory it," I say.

"Sounds like a plan."

I return to the convention hall confident that I have just won a bet. I go back to my constant chores of mapping. I make changes while I listen to a search and rescue team member tells me what he found that day. I have lunch and return, thinking I might have missed the delivery of the cases. I think of how quickly they came from Mt Weather and how slow they are to move the last 1,000 ft.

A fellow named Rick arrives and introduces himself to me. "I was over at the disaster field office at pier 90 and was ordered to report to you," he says. He is full of energy. "What can I do?" he asks.

I have only one laptop to produce maps and no place for him to sit. "Well, we have the equipment across the street in a warehouse and I'm waiting for it to arrive."

Rick gets excited. "One of those big GIS kits that come in boxes?" he asks.

"The same," I say.

"I got to put together one of those big plotters before. I'd like to try another," he says.

I start wondering why it hasn't been delivered yet. "Let's go across the street and check on it," I suggest.

The warehouse has changed, it's a busy place. There are now guards and marshals posted at the entrances. We are carded this time. After a few questions we are directed towards a man with a clipboard who is controlling the flow of goods in and out of the warehouse. He is surrounded by a small crowd, all talking to him at once, all telling him how important they are and how important it is for him to give them what they need immediately. Wrong approach. I feel sorry for him. We are all stressed and everything and everybody has a high priority.

Some of the important people move off and I go up to him and ask, "What kind of bribe would I have to give you to get these red cases moved across the street?"

51

Without waiting for reply Rick, standing beside me, says, "My knees have been dirty before."

I know instantly that I will like working with Rick.

The man with the clipboard is grateful for a ray of humor in an otherwise miserable day. "I was about to ship this stuff to the disaster field office on the pier," he says. I think instantly how if we hadn't showed up, we would have missed this opportunity to get it. I remind myself to stay on top of things during a disaster. "If you load it on a pallet I will have a forklift driver take it over to the convention center," he says. Rick and I quickly position pallets, place the cases on them, and use shrink-wrap to secure them. The forklift driver says he must finish unloading a truck full of water before he brings them over, but promises it will be the next thing he does.

On the way back I get to know Rick better. He is an ex cop, retired off the force. Twenty-five years of service. He tells me he has been shot, stabbed, beat up, spit upon, and anything else you can imagine could be done to a cop. He tells me he has spent time on the SWAT team. Now I know why he is a man of action. Once the equipment is delivered to our area, we set it up in record time. Usually the job takes four to six hours, even a whole day, but between the two of us we have it done in two hours. There is a hub, two workstations, two small color printers, a large plotter, and a server that can hold 150 gigs of data. He watches carefully how I plug wires in, and I can see he is curious about how it all fits together. He is hungry to learn, and he tells me he's still a novice GIS tech but he hopes to learn much from me while he's here.

Miraculously it all works and we are up and running. I immediately send large jobs to the plotter and begin printing out updated maps of the base of operations. Rick prints out a better GIS request form to help track requests and our production. We are overwhelmed by the demand for production. Search and rescue people want maps of the lower levels of the World Trade Center. Structural engineers want diagrams of the buildings. Safety officers would like locations of hazardous materials that were inside the building. There was a bank of backup batteries at the third level below the street, along with generators, used to keep the computers and networks in the building going twenty four hours a day. One of the buildings contained asbestos and they ask us if we know whether it was tower one or tower two. Another person requests the subway diagrams.

They patiently fill out the forms as I direct them. I tell them we will try to do it for them as soon as possible. They see we are overwhelmed. As a consolation prize we a set up a table with copies of everything we have produced. They scan the products, taking what they need.

Rick searches the Internet looking for GIS data on the web that will help us fill the requests. He finds some of the things we need. People bring things to GIS as well. Often it is raw data, hand drawings or marked up tourist maps that they want digitized and produced in large numbers or printed in big size on plotter paper. Often they are not the only ones who need that information. Someone shows up with a set of building plans and a side view diagram of the buildings and the sub floors. We do not have time to input it on the computer into GIS so we just make copies and put them out on our product table.

Greg comes back with Stavros. They both have that look, having witnessed the destruction first hand. They are somewhere between shock and desecration.

I try to cheer him up. "Check it out," I say, indicating the equipment. "What about the bet?"

He is happy to see all the equipment. "Not so fast," he says. "Was it here by 3:00?" he asks.

Rick smiles. "2:59," he says.

Greg knows the truth when he sees the results. He scans the maps on the product table. At least something is going right for him.

I'm beginning to notice more and more forest service people around. The size of this operation is increasing. Supplies are not the only thing arriving. A woman comes to me and asks if she can use my computer to access the Internet.

I have one of the few Internet connections available. Being one of the first responders on the site has its advantages. I was there when the telephone people were not as busy. Also some fellows from the City of New York came through one day setting up DSL service. I watched what they were doing and managed to get a few reserved IP addresses. Because of this I am able to download data and imagery from a secure ftp site. I can also search for other information. The woman needs to do research. She is a nurse or an EMT, I'm not sure which. She wears a forest service uniform. She is trying to get information about hazardous materials that the rescue workers may be encountering in the rubble. Again I hear that one of the main hazards is asbestos. Half of the first tower was built with this hazardous material before laws and building codes were changed. Another hazard is PCBs, a toxic compound that is used in electrical transformers. There was also a bank of batteries that served as a backup in the event of a power failure. The main hazard there is battery acid. Then there are medical hazards. Besides the usual tetanus, nobody knows what diseases could be mixed with the rubble.

Our humble GIS area,complete with deployed equipment.

She researches all this on the Internet. She prints out copies and prepares reports, her concern is not just the health of the search and rescue workers, but also everyone else here at this facility. She is grateful for the use of the computer. I talk to her a little bit more. She works in New Mexico at the Gila National Forest. I tell her about a visit I had to the Gila cliff dwellings once. I saw a bobcat right next to the road while driving on the long road leading to the visitor center. She tells me about some lakes in that area teeming with trout. Fishing seems to be one of her passions. We both agree that this is a beautiful country, full of little known parks and forests, pastoral back roads and countless scenic vistas.

I go back to work and begin updating maps again. I then begin working on a new request. One of the military commanders needs a map of all of the potential helicopter landing sites within 100 miles of Manhattan. I build a base map and begin to pull in data layers that may be appropriate. I query databases for schools with playgrounds. I look for baseball fields and recreational parks. Some buildings in my database are marked as having heliports on their rooftops. The soldier requesting the map tells me that by next week hundreds of helicopters will be around the city. The map will

help them locate emergency landing sites in the event of mechanical problems or the need for a quick evacuation.

The night wears on. I listen to the evening briefing as the rescuers report what they found and what has changed today at Ground Zero. They are very frustrated. You cannot remove debris and search at the same time, yet both are critical missions. While removing debris, the pile could shift and trap rescue workers that are underneath searching for survivors. The surrounding buildings have been diligently searched. The buildings have been cleared, a term used to designate just that. Attention is slowly turning back toward the pile that once was the World Trade Center. Somebody asks me if there were some way that I could get an estimate of the area that the debris fills. If the image were geographically registered I could trace the limits of the debris and draw a polygon. When you click on the completed polygon the software will automatically find the area of it. The problem is I have not registered the image. The process takes some time and involves choosing points on the image that correspond with real life points, things like street corners, tips of land, USGS benchmarks, and other features. Therein lies another problem. A lot of these features are buried under debris and it will be hard to accurately locate them. I tell him that I will get to it, writing it down and placing it on a growing pile of GIS requests.

Several men show up looking for me. "We're from the Minnesota Department of Natural Resources," they say. There are four of them. "We're GIS technicians. We have a trailer outside that is a mobile GIS mapping unit."

"The Mapmobile," pipes a second.

"We drove all night to get here," the first one explains.

"We've come to help," the second one says. "We are assigned to your unit."

Talk about the relief troops. I look over at the pile of GIS requests thinking how timely their arrival is. "What do you guys normally do?" I ask.

"We're sorry," one of them says. "We usually map forest fires and trees. We make large scale maps comprising thousands of acres of timber."

"We're mapping buildings here," I say. "The World Trade Center Plaza itself is only fourteen acres. My entire base of operations map comprises maybe 50 acres."

One of them says, "We've never mapped buildings, but we can sure try."

I like them already, they have the right attitude. I can tell that they are tired. I introduce them to Rick, the rest of the GIS

Staff at this point. "Why don't you get some rest and we'll help you get set up in the morning," I suggest.

Speaking of tired, it is midnight. Greg gives me the signal to wrap it up and get out of here. I am his ride to the hotel, so I do just that. Stavros rides with us, he's staying at the same place. They are talking about what they saw at Ground Zero today. Rescue workers have named points of interest to help them orient themselves in the massive pile of debris. There are places called the fingers, the rose bowl, the widow maker, and the supermarket. They want to start bringing maps forward with them every day and posting them at all the command centers.

They make cracks about my driving. I have driven in San Juan, Puerto Rico with the worst *tapon* in the world, and I have driven in New York City before. *El tapon* is the neck of the bottle, Puerto Rican for traffic jam. I put on my best New York accent and tell them I was sent to this disaster because I speak the language and can function as a translator. I teach them some simple New York phrases. If somebody asks "How you doing?" you say "Screw you. None of your business." I tell them to "quit bustin' my chops" and I make snide remarks at everything they say. They are impressed and I sound like a native New Yorker. It takes the edge off of the heavy conversation and loosens us all up before bed.

The fingers.

The potato chip

The Widowmaker

Sunday
September 16

I wake early after a restless sleep. I shower, dress, and go downstairs to request my car from valet parking. Greg shows up and tells me that Stavros will be coming in a little later and not to wait for him. We get in the car and I drive about a block where we are stopped in a traffic jam. A guy in a truck pulls next to us and spots our FEMA badges as he looks over. He tells us that he would like to give us a bunch of doughnuts. He is grateful that FEMA is here and helping his city. We graciously accept the doughnuts and he hands us 20 boxes tied together with string in two big bundles. It is much more than we expected.

We continue driving to work. This time I spot a parking place in front of the building. Greg is tired of walking great distances to the car each night. I pull in the spot but a policeman comes over and tells us it is restricted. Greg quickly announces that he is the situation branch chief, displaying his FEMA badge. The policemen says OK. I hand him a box of doughnuts and thank him.

The two policemen at the next security checkpoint smell the donuts. I'm not trying to stereotype, but these guys lit up at the mere sight of the boxes, even though they are unmarked. I am suddenly short two more boxes. My trip to my work area continues pretty much the same, passing out more donuts along the way until I finally arrive at my workstation with only two boxes left. I open one up and see the largest, most fantastic doughnuts I have ever seen. Each box held only six or eight, not a dozen as I had thought; they were that big! Oh well, I didn't need the calories anyway. They feed us quite well here. I get little egg omelets in the morning with hash browns and biscuits or toast, and there are juices, bagels, milk, cereal, and fruit to choose from as well. The Red Cross feeds us too from a mobile food truck parked in a secure area outside. One day I went out there for a hamburger and Loretta Swit, famous for playing "Hot Lips" on the television series M.A.S.H., smiled back at me from inside the truck. She cooked a damn fine burger.

The Minnesota guys are up early and raring to go. They want to know where to park their trailer so we scout around until we find somewhere suitable. They bring it inside the building but cannot locate close to us. They wind up parking way in the back by the loading dock. Once they are set up I meet with them briefly. Two of them are going to work the night shift and the other two will take the day. I give them a few requests that need work. I ask them if they can import and georeference the aerial imagery of the World Trade Center. I have also tasked them with digitizing the basements and sub floors from the architectural plans someone has provided. One of them humbly explains to me that he is diabetic and he shows me his monitoring kit. I've to tell him it's OK, I keep plenty of snacks and juice around, pointing to their junk food near my workstation.

The day wears on. Rick and I are busy working and dealing with the constant requests for information. The convention center is getting crowded as more and more people arrive to support the rescue operations. Several new forest service guys have arrived to work in our department. Greg has requested them. He calls them DPROs, another acronym. I don't know what it means, maybe display processors. They are normally GIS technicians but they say they are glad to be here and have the opportunity to help. I show them our map-making system using MapInfo. They are familiar with ArcView, the competitive GIS software. It helps to know both and I tell them they are welcome to try any time they want. Many of the FEMA GIS Technicians I have worked with know both systems. We do a lot of conversions between software when we share information with other agencies.

We have a small GIS meeting. "Don't worry too much about being 100% accurate," I tell them. "In a normal GIS environment that would be the main goal. In this case, time is of the essence. Delaying the release of a map because of an error would be a mistake. The maps we are creating are crucial to supporting the operation. Life is at stake.

"These building footprints, for example. I heard someone had the data layers for the buildings, and they told me that they were going to get them for me. I'd still be waiting without anything to show if I hadn't drawn the building footprints freehand from a tourist map. Later on, if and when I do get the real thing, I will replace my crude data and update the maps. As someone said to me: Don't worry about the building footprint being accurate, there are no buildings there anymore."

That night the guys realize exactly what I am talking about. They are listening to the debriefing. Tonight it is their turn to hear what was found and where. I can't help but overhear, since I work nearby. One of the workers is explaining about how a cone of body parts was found on the rooftop of a building on the opposite side of the tower where the airplane entered. "They didn't come from the Tower," he tells us. "We believe these are pieces of the people that were in the airplane."

I hear him say something I didn't know. "Each piece that they find goes in its own body bag." Now I understand why 30,000 were ordered and why this may not be enough.

"I found a piece of hair today attached to a scalp on a rooftop," he says, pointing to a building on a big aerial photo that we have laid out on the table. "This is somebody's loved one. It may take time to figure out who it is, depending on whether or not they have a DNA record, but to somebody waiting for news it is proof that their loved one is gone."

I am thinking. So many people are missing, so many people are in doubt. Where have all the people gone? I am hiding my

Compaction: Fallen layers of collapsed concrete and building compressed beyond recognition.

head in the computer monitor again.

As if listening to my thoughts one of other guys from Minnesota asks him, "Where have all the people gone?"

They have probably all been burned," he says. "The smoke rising from the rubble of the World Trade Center contains the ashes of the victims. I'll bet we don't find anybody in the pile. Maybe the firemen or the policemen that were around it when it collapsed, but not anyone from the offices inside the building. If there is anybody to find they are probably underneath in the tunnels of the subway or the mall, trapped in voids."

"What are voids?" asks someone.

"Small open areas inside the debris. In an earthquake, for instance, the building shakes from side to side. When it collapses one side will slip off the pilings and fall, creating a little triangle,

an air pocket we call a void. These are the places we find survivors. Any open space inside the collapsed debris is called a void."

My thoughts are interrupted by the appearance of a tall thin man wearing a FEMA badge. He introduces himself as Rob. I'm glad to meet him. We have worked together on several occasions but have never met face to face. He tells me that Franklin, another man I have never met face to face yet worked closely with, is on his way. Rob is regular FEMA, a full timer who works in a west coast office. We are stretched few and far between and there are not enough FEMA people to go around. He's excited about what he finds going on here at the convention center. He has just come from visiting GIS at the other FEMA office and says it is not nearly as busy.

"Give it time," I say. The DFO, Disaster Field Office, is there for the long haul. He scans our piles of maps and products and is pleased with what he finds. He studies the aerial image of the World Trade Center that we have been pointing to and talking about in our briefings. In the photograph the debris pile spreads in all directions and a smoky plume pushes up from a dark crater in the center. Trucks can be seen lined up waiting to be loaded with debris.

Rob tells me that he has come to help coordinate and liaise between the numerous operating GIS units. I had already known about the fire department operating on pier 92 and the FEMA operation on pier 90. I had also seen maps coming from a GIS unit somewhere in New Jersey. Rob will help with the exchange of data and with the sharing of maps so we are not duplicating efforts. I give him a shopping list of data and tell him what I have to offer in exchange. I imagine lots of ArcView data conversions in my near future.

At this time in the disaster I am well networked, not just with computer equipment but also with connections everywhere in this facility. Being personable and service oriented has its advantages in this business. Plus I have supply sergeant mentality when it comes to supplying my customers with product. I am always on the lookout for things that I need to get my job done and to increase my service levels. For example, earlier today one of our plotters had run out of ink and my supply of paper was low. After delivering the helicopter-landing map for the National Guard they were more than pleased to return the favor. They went out and bought me some ink and paper on their budget, glad to pitch in where needed.

The National Guard Military Police have a tough mission. Their job is to patrol the sectors downtown and help secure the area. The sergeant in charge tells me that people have been looting. Some have been going into the empty office buildings around the

World Trade Center and stealing computers and equipment. Some of the bars and restaurants have reported liquor missing. He tells me that during a disaster like this the National Guard Military Police have the same authority as U.S. Marshals. I realize that there are many laws in place that govern different authorities during a disaster. It can create some complicated issues.

FEMA is just what the name says, a management agency. Their job is to provide guidance and funding where needed. It is the State, or in this case the City, that is really in charge. In particular, it is the New York City Fire Department that is in charge of the rescue operation at Ground Zero. We all work for them.

Suddenly there is a commotion in the hall. A small four-wheeled quad is driving in circles up and down the aisles. This is the latest piece of equipment to arrive. "Nice toy," somebody mutters but the MP says it will be a valuable asset down at Ground Zero.

"At least it's more comfortable than a HumVee," I say. I have been given a ride in those metal boxes once too often. "Comfortable," I mutter, "But not by much."

Rob meets Greg and asks him what he needs. Greg complains to him about not having any pencils, yet here these people go and get this stupid motorcycle. "Where are the priorities here?" he says. I can tell he's tired. Stavros is too, and so is Rick. Rick walks through the city every night to Grand Central Station where he catches the last train leaving towards wherever he is staying. From his conversation I gather it is not close to this facility. I tell him we will be leaving shortly and I offer to give him a ride if he wants one.

Greg has a severe dawdle factor, as I like to call it. Stavros makes a comment about it. We are all ready to go, yet Greg stops on his way out to talk to over a dozen people. Rick finally gives up and heads off into the city. He is worried about missing the last train. Stavros and I razz Greg in our best New York accents. It seems to work. He gets the message and catches up to us.

On the way home Greg tries to talk Stavros into going out for a while. He wants some company so I agree to go with him. I park at the hotel, go upstairs, change shirts, and meet him back downstairs in the lobby. He knows a place we can walk to around the corner. We go out into Times Square. I don't ever recall it looking this empty. I realize that it is Sunday night and it's after midnight, but there are only 30 or 40 people in the whole square. We pass by some skinny hookers. Word is they are giving half off to rescue workers. I eye one of them, unsure if it is a man in drag or a woman. Greg remarks, "Everyone has their purpose in life." I like his attitude. He is a true people person.

We pass idle conversation at the bar as I learn more about the man I work with. He loves to travel. He tells me about some fantastically cheap trips he has taken around the world. He is full of interesting conversation and I am glad I decided to get out tonight, even though I am tired and less than six hours away from going back to work. He has worked in Saudi Arabia and we discuss cultural and religious differences. He tells me about Saudi Arabian soap operas which all have the same plot involving righteous, militant Arabs and evil, conspiring Jews.

He tells me about a time he was rescued from a Dutch island in a daring airlift following hurricane Luis in the Caribbean. He lost a sailboat in that one. Luis was one week before Hurricane Marilyn, the disaster that landed me inside FEMA. I begin to see how much we really have in common.

After a while I am extremely tired. I wish I could stay and listen to more, but I know tomorrow will come quickly. We both need our rest. We walk back across the empty Times Square, and I wonder if it is empty because the city contains that many less people now. I dream of 20,000 missing persons that night, looking for them on the empty streets of New York City.

I am looking everywhere. It is night and the streets are empty. The lights are on and on some of the light posts I see missing signs with pictures of the people I am searching for. I look up from one of the pictures and finally find one of the men whose picture I had just seen. He looks at me with empty eyes, an air of heaviness surrounds him like a shroud. "It is time to move on," he says.

World Trade Center, Before and After September 11, 2001

Monday
September 17

    I ask one of the forest service fellows today what they do with GIS during a forest fire. I am curious about what maps they produce. They say the first map that they always make offers three scenarios: a worst case, best case, and middle ground. The maps help firefighters draw lines of defense. Sometimes they will choose an area and back burn into the fire as a way of controlling it. This map is updated frequently. One of the guys on the team is qualified to do aerial imagery. He travels with special cameras and often flies over the burning forest photographing the extent of the flames. This image can become a base map for the next operational period, showing the burned areas and the locations of assets like trucks and equipment. To make it more useful, the photograph is registered geographically. Data layers containing forest service roads, highways, buildings, towers, and other features are added to the maps and labeled.

When they are not putting out fires they often create maps of timber stands. Using infrared photography they can tell what types of trees are prevalent in a given forest. Once again I'm amazed at how flexible they are and how they have been able to adapt their skills to this situation and focus on a few square miles when they are used to thousands of acres.

I get a call from Washington. They tell me that Rob is on his way, the same Rob that arrived last night. Rob is already sitting in the corner. After hanging up the phone I go over to him. "Good news from Washington," I say. "Rob is on his way."

He laughs. "I left before getting final authorization," he says. "I had the feeling it would be too late if I waited. I knew that the paperwork would catch up eventually. Makes me feel a little relieved."

"I know," I say. "I have heard stories about people being asked to leave the disaster and return home at their own expense."

"I have, too," says Rob. "There's a memo to that respect circulating over at the pier," he says. "People have been coming up and reporting without authorization."

Like most disaster workers I don't think about the expense. Government reimbursement has never equaled my expenses, it seems there is always something trivial being denied and the paperwork to do a reclaim is horrendous. I have lost premium pay, had per-diem down rated, and forgotten to include legitimate expenses. I think the majority of people here are using their personal cell phones for government business because supplies of them have not yet arrived.

"How did you get here anyway?" I ask.

"We drove."

"From the west coast?!!" I say.

"When we heard about it, me and two others just got in a car and drove cross-country to get here."

"I guess nothing was flying yet," I say.

"Yeah, we could have waited around a few days and checked or hoped if there were any flights. Instead we jammed ourselves in a car full of suitcases and took off. Franklin was with me on an assignment out there," he says. "Since he works for the mapping and analysis center we had to take him directly to Washington. His paperwork is a little different and he could not come directly here without risking some disciplinary action."

"Headquarters sometimes functions a little different than the regions," I say. I am glad I came the legitimate way through an authorized deployment. My Region goes by the book at least.

"It was fun," continues Rob. "We weren't thinking of where we were going, and we knew it would be serious when we got here. We laughed all the way across the country to pass the time. Whenever the driver got tired he pulled off and somebody else took his place. It was dark when we passed the sign that announced we were crossing the Mississippi River, but we stopped and looked anyway."

"What did it look like?" I asked.

"There was nothing to see. It was dark and the middle of the night. We looked around for a minute and got back in the car and continued the trip."

"Sounds like fun," I said.

"Pretty much was. My tour of the country, like college kids on spring break."

Back to work. Greg and Stavros have been taking pictures documenting Ground Zero. Stavros is trying to offload them out of the digital camera so he can to clear some disk space before he heads downtown again.

Next to me behind a stack of transit cases is a telecommunications specialist who works with search and rescue. He is also a fireman. His job is to keep all their radios in operation. He also sets up transmission towers that broadcast signals. He has taken many pictures of Ground Zero. I arrange to have his computer hooked into our network where I download his pictures onto a local disk. I have all the documentation pictures that Stavros

has been taking at the site. Other firemen bring me pictures as well and I find that GIS has become a repository for these images.

Some of the search and rescue teams are preparing to demobilize. I cut CDs for their memories. Greg tells me these things will be valuable one day, like maps and pictures of Pearl Harbor are today. We all have our small piece of history. When word gets around about the CDs, I begin to worry. I do not have time to burn CDs all day, but people are nice about it. They bring blank CDs, always more than they want, so I have the supplies to make extras. Kinkos agrees to cut the CDs for me if I make one master copy. I want to do a good job, to put my web development skills to work and make a professional CD, but I do not have the time. I wind up creating a set of simple directories containing the pictures.

Kinkos has become invaluable. FEMA does not have a badge-making machine on site yet. Kinkos personnel have set up a station where incoming people can be badged with proper

credentials. Security is ever alert. They already caught someone trying to sneak in with false credentials. They did not have the Kinkos made badge, but a homemade FEMA badge. Someone spotted it quickly. The official badge has a funny watermark and it is hard to counterfeit. The impostor even dressed like a search and rescue team member in full gear. There is no word about what he might have been up to, but he was quickly arrested and our security was doubled. We are ever diligent in these operations, but somehow we always worry that it is not enough.

The Governor of Puerto Rico came to have lunch with us today. She was very personable and enjoyed meeting us. Having lived in Puerto Rico I have a special place in my heart for her and for the Puerto Rican people. I have never met a warmer and friendlier people. After Hurricane Marilyn when my wife was in distress, they took good care of her. They know hardship and they know what affect a hurricane can have on a person's psyche. I left Puerto Rico after living there for two years. After I left I received a thank you note from one of the officials in the government there. His words, in addition to being warm hearted, simply said that I would always have a *hermano* there.

Since that time I have been back to Puerto Rico twice to help with hurricane relief efforts. I am glad to see a search and rescue team from Puerto Rico represented here.

Randy arrived today. I have worked with him before as well. He's a genius at networking, a Novell CNE, Microsoft Certified System Engineer, and Cisco certified as well. I unpack and put the network together, hooking up wires and plugging in machines. It is miraculous that it works after being packed and unpacked so many times per year. I get it up and running, but Randy tunes it and makes its sing. He had to go to the other FEMA office first. They are having problems getting their server to run. He says he will be back soon as there is much more to do here. He too is the type of individual who enjoys the front lines.

Another plotter arrives, along with a large laser printer capable of printing on indestructible paper. One problem with our paper maps is they fall apart in the conditions at Ground Zero. This printer burns the image on special paper that cannot be torn or faded by water. As a test, everyone tries to rip it but no one can succeed.

Randy is challenged setting up this printer. There are problems at first but he quickly irons them out. It has been a long day for him but he works tirelessly. He does not stop to eat until everything is functioning and he is sure the network is operating to his satisfaction. He knows that his time here is short and he knows that he has two more networks to tune on this deployment so he works twice as hard. He tries to network in the Minnesota guys and their mapmobile, but they are too far away and we have exceeded the limitations of network cabling. It did not stop him from trying. Once again it is a long day with everybody pulling hard for success in their individual jobs. I can't think of a finer, more dedicated group and it is sad to think about the final disposition of all this talent. Once everything is running smooth these disaster teams are usually disbanded and sent home. It's the nature of the business, until next time, and God forbid that we should need such an organization like this so soon again.

An eerie sight: South Manhattan with no World Trade Center in
the skyline.

Tuesday
September 18

The Minnesota guys on the night shift have done a fantastic
job. With more people arriving to help with GIS, the quality of
products has gone up. They have made beautiful maps using the
imagery as a base layer for all their maps. It gives every map a
sense of realism that cannot be seen in my simple line maps. They
have also digitized the sub floors the World Trade Center. Their
mission now is to update these maps as the some sub floors are
breached and searched. We have chosen color schemes to indicate

areas that are cleared and areas that have yet to be searched. The maps give anyone an instant picture of where we are in search and rescue operations around the collapsed towers.

The buildings surrounding the World Trade Center are slowly being searched and cleared as well. Searching them is an arduous task. There are no elevators, no electricity, and no lights. The urban search and rescue teams climb sometimes 40 or 50 stories through dark stairwells searching each floor and each office. They look carefully under desks and move furniture. They move fallen ceiling tiles and look under small debris piles, leaving no stone unturned, as the expression goes. One of them describes the passage up one of the buildings to me. He tells me that it is one of the strangest things he has ever seen. The bottom five or ten floors are in pretty good shape. The middle floors are all charred and burnt. He shows me a picture of a melted bicycle next to a blackened concrete wall and a broken window, saying that this was on one of those floors. Once you get above 30 or 40 floors everything is normal again, except for the broken glass and the fallen ceiling tiles.

A man named Brandon has joined the team. He is an EMT with the forest service and usually does wilderness search and rescue. He and several others are going downtown to Ground Zero and he asks me to come along. The unit is running smooth, and Greg has ordered everyone to go down there at least once to see what we are dealing with. I worked a disaster in Texas where they made us all visit a recovery center and drive through some of the damaged areas of Houston. I saw a lady crying on her porch in an area that had been inundated by flood waters. Her house was near a neighborhood sewage tank. The tank had overflowed and raw sewage had flowed in her back door and out the front. The house was a shambles.

Refrigerated trucks and the ambulance staging area.

The pile continues to smolder and burn long after September 11.

We are required to wear safety equipment: long sleeve jackets, hard hats, and dust masks. Carbon filtered masks are optional but are recommended because of the rank smell. I gather these things quickly along with bottled water and my digital camera. We head out the back door to a dock across the street, drawing stares from ferry passengers and commuters. There we board an Army Corps of Engineers boat that will transport us downtown. This is a vast improvement over driving. Traffic on the waterways is significantly less than on the streets, but still it is crowded.

Before heading south we must first go to the other FEMA location at pier 90 where we will pick up more passengers. I recognize one of them immediately, having served with him during Hurricane Marilyn, another temporary organization that was disbanded long ago. We pass the time chattering.

"If necessary, FEMA is ready to help pay to rebuild the World Trade Center," he says.

"Will be taller than the last World Trade Center?" asks Brandon.

"I can't say," he replies.

"Stories about rebuilding the towers are already in the media," I say. "I hear Donald Trump, one of New York wealthiest developers, has already submitted a plan."

"I don't think it's right to rebuild there," says one of the fellows with us. There is some brisk debate on whether it is right or wrong to rebuild on that site.

"People have mixed feelings," I say, giving my opinion. "Ultimately I feel that New York City will not let the real estate value of that property go undeveloped."

"Right," says my friend. "They lost over 15% of the office space in this disaster. Some businesses have already relocated across the river in New Jersey."

We approach south Manhattan, my first view since exiting the ramp towards the Lincoln Tunnel. It's not the same as seeing it through aerial photographs, but it is just as stark and shocking. Once again, instead of the familiar towers, a plume of smoke rises from where the tall buildings once stood. We debark at the ferry terminal behind the World Financial Center. This was the site where thousands of people were evacuated to New Jersey following the collapse of the Towers. I can only imagine what it must have looked like, the site of the collapsed and burning towers, the destruction, and the horror as people were ferried to safety. I imagine that Lot's wife of Biblical fame must have witnessed a similar scene as she turned to stare at the destruction behind her.

Search and rescue dogs wear safety gear when they work, too.

Fire Truck Alley where they towed all the destroyed fire trucks that were dug from under the rubble. A lot of emergency equipment was lost.

86

Collateral Damage

    We begin our trek by walking north one block along the water, turning right onto Vessy Street. I finally get a glimpse at some of the facilities that I have been mapping. The temporary morgue looks nothing like I imagined. It is a mobile home trailer. There is green astro-turf carpet in front of the door. Two large flowerpots stand on either side of the entrance. It has the air and appearance of a mobile funeral parlor, very dignified. Off to the side and not far away is a line of refrigerated trucks.

    Further down the street is an ambulance staging area. Drivers and EMT's wait nervously for customers that may never come. On their dashboards I spy maps that I have produced. These maps show the fastest routes to the nearest hospitals with little arrows indicating one-way streets. Three National Guardsmen wearing masks sit outside the doorway of the American Express Building that stands on the corner behind the ambulances. There are red spray paint marks on the side of the building, a large X. This is the symbol left behind by a search and rescue team indicating that the building has been cleared. Each side of the open x contains a written piece of information. The date is written on top, followed clockwise by the number of survivors found inside, the number of bodies recovered, and the team that conducted the search.

At the corner of Vessy and West I get my first glimpse of the debris. This place is like a giant construction site. Heavy equipment and men move about in all directions. The beep of large machines in reverse is heard everywhere along with the gunning of diesel engines. Tall cranes lift and drop debris into waiting dump trucks. On the opposite corner a Red Cross worker is offering

snacks and bottled water to the emergency workers. Occasionally someone walks by with a bucket of ice filled with bottled water. It is hot outside. I ask Brandon if it is necessary to wear the dust mask. I do not see many other people wearing them, especially the construction workers. Brandon asks me if I have any allergies. I say no. He says it is a matter of preference. There is a funny smell in the air and an aftertaste I cannot describe. It is not just the dust, there is a pervasive smell like burning plastic, with an odd overtone that cannot be identified. I secure my mask again, deciding I prefer the relative safety it offers.

We can go no further on Vessy Street, the debris of a collapsed building designated only as World Trade Center Seven blocks the way. We turn north on West Street and walk several blocks. I pass the emergency Veterinarian hospital. It is little more than a tent, as are most of these facilities that I have been mapping. A hand drawn sign outside indicates that it is a hospital. I meet a rescue worker and her dog. The dog is wearing little boots to protect his paws from lacerations inflicted by walking on the debris.

Further north we come upon a much larger tent, the base of operations. Inside the tent on a plywood stand I see one of my large maps posted. There is a trailer parked next to the tent. It is air-conditioned. I imagine it to be a welcome haven from the noise and the smell and the dust outside.

We turn down Chambers Street, the first place clear enough to cut through. Some of the signposts have been twisted so that the streets are mis-marked. On the ground is a thick layer of muddy material, like clay mixed with concrete. It covers the walls of the surrounding buildings as well. People write in it like they would on the windows of dirty cars, except the messages are to missing loved ones and fallen comrades.

I drink my bottle of water. It is hot. I walk over to an open trashcan and toss the bottle in, but I miss. Instead it falls on the street. I bend down and pick it up trying a second time to unsuccessfully throw it into the wastebasket. A Red Cross lady standing nearby shakes her head and smiles. There is trash everywhere on the ground and my effort is laughable if not pathetic.

At the next corner we come to Greenwich Street. Looking south, debris fills the street. It has been partially cleared but it is still impassable. The light posts are covered with small paper signs  taped all around them. They are the signs I saw people making at Kinkos, the pleas to find missing loved ones. All of them have photographs of a person in a happier time, some with their pets, some with other people. Each contains the key word "MISSING", usually at the top of the page.

There is a trash dumpster nearby, the words "FBI Airplane parts" are spray painted on the side. There are not many parts in the dumpster, at least not an entire airplane. There are pictures posted of what the airplane's black box looks like with instructions of who to notify if it is found. It is not a black box as I've always thought it would be, it is a red cylinder.

The subway entrances that have been cleared of debris are visible and boarded over to block access. Many of the buildings around the site have the red X mark of the search and rescue team that cleared the building. Most of the ground level stores are boarded up. Glass hangs above us and there are many unsuspecting hazards. It is natural to look side to side but now I must train myself to look up continually and make sure that I am not standing under some debris precariously perched above my head and ready to fall.

We turn down Church Street passing in front of Borders Bookstore where less than six months ago I shopped with my son. Looking up at what remains of the building I see a giant steel girder sticking out of the side about five stories up. I turn and move forward into what was once the World Trade Center Plaza but is

 now a junkyard. I follow a small footpath through the debris to a position where, in better times, I could have stood and admired the tall buildings and the majestic fountain up close. The golden ball, once the centerpiece of the fountain, lies damaged atop a pile of twisted

metal, a large dent in the formerly perfect sphere. I walk out on a concrete beam and look down through collapsed concrete slabs into what used to be the mall under the plaza. It was here, after shopping with my son, we went to Victoria's Secret and bought my wife a gift. Now I stare down into a rubble pile. Below me, dropping a few feet, there is another small footpath winding through the debris. It leads to a hole where a day-glow orange arrow indicates the entrance to the underground mall, a portal now used only by the search and rescue teams. The hole is barely large enough for an individual to squeeze through. It is dark beyond that. I begin to get an appreciation of why the maps are so valuable. My son and I got lost in the mall when we were here. Having been here before, I see no point of reference to focus on and orient myself. I can't even make sense of what I am seeing.

I walk back to Church Street. On the corner is a crude first aid station. I had cut myself unpacking the GIS equipment a few days ago and I get a fresh bandage and some topical antibiotic. I tell myself to be careful, unknown diseases may be lurking everywhere in this debris.

All the buildings around the plaza are scarred. All have broken windows and pieces of debris lodged in their sides. I see the "building with the gash" or the "widowmaker" as they call it. It looks as if it was a piece of plastic and someone ran a hot poker or a soldering iron up the smooth side of the building and cut into it. It reminds me of cut away diagrams I used to look at in books when I was a kid. Some of the faces of the buildings are missing, making them appear like dollhouses, the furniture exposed to the open air. Paper litters the street, if you can call it a street. It is little more than a dark, trampled ash pile compacted under the weight of men and machinery. There are no curbs to be found. Occasionally a piece of sidewalk is visible, but only after you move away from the plaza. Across this layer of ash are laid giant power cables that lead to banks of lights used to illuminate the area at night with artificial daylight.

There is a small cemetery at the corner of Church and Vessy. It is the only place completely free of debris. Reverence for the dead runs high in this place. If not for the macabre surroundings this cemetery would appear peaceful and normal.

I take some pictures of the hanging debris above us, one of my reasons for coming here. We should be mapping the safety hazards, but there are so many we would quickly run out of map room. On one wall I see a large, spray painted arrow indicating to look up, the warning "GLASS" written beside it. I look up and see a piece of a picture window jutting out from the building. I wonder what is holding it in place.

Bob points to a corner of the World Trade Center Tower Two that is still standing. At first I think it is the corner of the building but I realize it is out of place. It is actually a piece of the building which fell and planted itself vertically in the ground. He tells me this is the debris feature that the rescue people call the fingers. It almost looks like two hands held open side by side. I spy the radio tower that was at the top of Tower One. It is sticking pointed side down in the smoldering ground like a broken tiki torch. This place defies your imagination. You cannot imagine, you cannot fathom, your senses are overwhelmed when you witness this much destruction. I cannot recall having even seen a junkyard that resembles this, but that would be a starting point. There is nothing to describe it, and pictures do not do it justice. I would hear many people try to describe it in such words, but we have no words because we have never witnessed anything like this in the history of mankind.

On the corner of Liberty is an Operations Center stationed inside a firehouse. Ten hook ten it is called. I have heard that the people from this fire station were called to another fire and were not in the building at the time the planes hit the towers. I do not know if that is true, but it was a blessing in disguise. For those stationed here there are feelings of unworthiness, these heroes feel guilty and undeserving. This twist of fate saved them from what would have otherwise been their battle to fight. I almost think they would rest easier beneath the pile of debris with their fallen comrades. I understand these feelings of unworthiness and guilt. I have them myself although I can't exactly tell you why. What right do we have to go on living when so many have senselessly died? Why them over us? In my dreams I sometimes share their doomed company. I know I am not alone in these terrible dreams. I have heard others talk about similar nightmares.

Policemen move in and out of the building busily going about their tasks. On the west side of the street is a barricade. Behind it I see a priest. I stop to talk to him. He tells me his Parrish is as at Times Square and that he has come down here to comfort people.

A priest stares into the soul of terrorism seeking an answer to this malevolence.

He says this act of terrorism was evil and he wants to gain firsthand experience so he can preach about it in his sermons. "This is evil," he says. "I would damn their souls if I could." His religion and his status in his faith forbid it. One evil does not justify another, and as a priest, his life is an example for others to follow. He asks me if he can go see it, if he can get a closer look at it. I escort him to the edge of the pile. He looks at its sadly and says, "This is a grave." Then he blesses it. I don't know if it is habit, but I make the sign of the cross. I take his picture and give him my business card. I tell him to email me and I will send him the pictures. I return him to the barricade where I met him.

101

103

We can't get all the way down Liberty Street, it is blocked by debris so we head south one more block to cross back toward the water on the south side of the pile. Each corner of this mess has been like the first, a flurry of activity between construction equipment and men. Occasionally I see a welder with a torch cutting larger pieces of steel into smaller ones so they can be placed on trucks and hauled away. As I walk west I pass a fireman sitting on a concrete block. His face rests in his hands and he looks tired. It is obvious he has been crying and is trying to hide. I wonder if I look as obvious when I bury my head in the computer monitor. On another corner I spot another fireman with a shirt that says "The new Twin Towers." It is a picture of a policeman and a fireman standing together in the rubble roughly where the twin towers would be. I ask him where he got the shirt and he tells me someone has dropped a box of them off at every fire station in town.

I look north up Washington Street towards the Trade Center. There I can see a thirteen-story piece of the building, the corner of Tower Two. We continue walking another block until we are back at West Street. Most of this area has been cleared to gain access. I find myself watching a large crane carefully load a 40 or 50 ft. piece of twisted steel onto a flatbed truck. I can only imagine what it must have sounded like as this metal strained and broke free of the building. It is huge, at least four inches thick. I see many such pieces in the debris field, dwarfed by the size of the pile, lost in a morass of destruction.

One block north on West, I come to the overhead walkway, the one that miraculously remains standing. It goes across the road and ends abruptly on the southwest corner of West and Liberty Street where the Greek Orthodox Church once stood. I can't tell that there was ever a church there. I can't tell that there was anything there but an empty lot full of rubble.

We rest in the shade underneath what is left of the walkway. A survey team has a laser beam trained on the corner of what remains of Tower Two. I ask them what they are doing. They tell me they are monitoring the movement of the tower. If it moves too far they will sound a warning and tell people to get back. It could collapse at any moment. Again I wonder how hard it will be to cut that up into little pieces and load it on trucks.

Bob calls me the ambassador of good will. He tells me they should have sent me here every day. I have talked and interacted with people, trying to lift spirits, but I am no ambassador. I am minutes away from caving in. We stand there in the shade fifteen or twenty minutes just staring at all. It is hard to fathom and even harder to explain. Again, pictures do not do it justice. Think of the most fantastic vista of scenery, a view of a beautiful valley from a glistening mountaintop. It takes your breath away and you drink in the scenery from all directions, surrounded by nature in its glory. Now twist that scenery around in the something ugly and evil, something unnatural. Imagine the dirtiest place you have ever been, the filthiest junkyard, the most disgusting abandoned building. Add to it a smell, burning plastic and rotting garbage. You're not even close but you are beginning to move in the right direction.

We are tired from all the walking. It is as an effort to trudge through this mess. Across the street near what was once the Marriott Hotel I see the famous bucket brigade. Men are passing five gallon plastic buckets partially filled with dirt and debris. They do this until they are tired. A steady stream of reserves waits nearby to take the place of any man who tires and can lift no more.

A five story American flag hangs proudly from the side of one of the buildings of the World Financial Center. There are American flags flying from the booms of the cranes. Debris trucks also have flags tied to their antennas or taped to their doors. Americans are always at their best in the worst moments. I'm proud to be an American.

I've seen enough.

We work our way back to the ferry dock and call for the boat to pick us up. It is hot and we remove our hard hats now that we are away from the site. People are beginning to conglomerate at the ferries, catching the afternoon commute home across the river. Wall Street was recently opened again. Business as usual.

In the small lagoon I see a Manhattan Island tour boat circle around, offering the passengers a glimpse of the smoking debris. I am reminded of rubber-neckers at the scene of an accident. It is human nature to have this morbid curiosity. I'm no different. As the counselors will tell me later during my debriefings, I am only human.

Wednesday
September 19

    Like most people who work for a FEMA, I have a technique for dealing with stress. I focus on the task at hand and try not to think about the job. It worked at Rio Piedras to a point. The dots on the maps became just that: simple dots. As long as they remained dots I was okay. When I would stop and realize that they represent bodies, more properly souls, I began to break down. I have been going through that scenario for a number of days now and have managed to hide my sorrow well. Greg recognizes it. He keeps asking me if I'm OK, and I keep telling him I'm fine, but he knows better.

    I can see the light at the end of the tunnel. I know I'm going home soon. Something I have not mentioned. My uncle died a few days ago. He was my favorite uncle and he used to baby-sit me when I was young. I have been so busy that I feel like I haven't had time to stop and accept the loss. I went to see him in early July when he was still sick in the hospital with cancer. I think I achieved some closure at that time, but I'm not really sure. I kept telling myself I would go see him again before he passed on, and I believed that there would always be time to do that. Sometimes I forget that nobody lives forever, or maybe I would like to believe we are all immortal, allotted with enough time on the cosmic clock in which to complete everything we want to accomplish in life. My wife says I live in a dream world. I also believe in Utopian societies, that peace on Earth can exist, and that somewhere inside every person there is some good. At least I can say I believed those things before September 11. When I get the time I plan on reevaluating my beliefs, just as everyone in this country is probably doing.

Anyway, my mother moved into my uncle's house to take care of him. She told me how sick he was, how he couldn't eat, and how he was slowly wasting away. The end for him I believe was welcome, at least he is no longer suffering. I was planning on staying until next Monday, but now I have learned that my entire family will be at the funeral on Saturday. I should be there.

Where are my feelings for my uncle? I grieve more for the souls lost in the World Trade Center disaster than I do for my own kin. Perhaps it is because death was welcome in his case. Nobody on those airplanes that collided with the World Trade Center had a death wish except perhaps the terrorists. Given the opportunity I'm sure they all would have chosen life.

Another twist to the details in this story: the death of my uncle has given me a way out. I am free to leave, released because of personal tragedy. If not for this turn of events I would have a problem. I would be here for weeks I imagine, at least until the first week of October when this convention center is scheduled to be shut down and everyone here will be sent home. In my mind I balance and weigh everything, my need to return to work before I lose my job at home, my desire to be with my family again, and my willingness to help in this terrible disaster. And now my uncle's death is added to that. I know what I must do, what is the right thing to do. I will be home in a few days.

Two new guys arrive on the scene. One of them announces that he is my replacement. He announces his title with flair. I get the impression that he is arrogant and a bit cocky, but if he's good it doesn't really matter. Before learning anything about what we're doing he decides to take a trip down to the site. He leaves before I have a chance to talk to him. I get the impression that he is not interested in anything I have to say anyway.

Greg has told me to make sure I schedule myself to debrief. He tells me a little bit about the sessions that the search and rescue guys go through when they finish every mission. He tells me how good they are and how healthy and helpful. Since a lot of the units are beginning to go home I have an opportunity to talk with them.

I wonder if these sessions do more harm than good. I begin to hear things that I never would have heard. Many of the men relate their experience at the World Trade Center to the Oklahoma City Bombing that occurred on April 19, 1995.

"I was on one of the last teams sent to Oklahoma City," one man explains. "By the time my team had arrived there were no longer any victims to be found, no one left to rescue, only remains to be recovered. It was nothing like this convention center. We had comfortable rooms to sleep in with curtains on the windows. The rooms were filled with cots, the same kind of cots we sleep on here in the convention center, except instead of military issue blankets they were made up with real sheets and homemade comforters. On every cot was a teddy bear with a note saying thank you for being here."

"I was there, too," says another man, joining in the conversation. "The work was hard." He becomes emotional at this point. "I was working the site and I found a hand, a perfectly manicured hand protruding from the rubble. It was a woman's hand, the nails painted bright red with a Timex watch around the wrist that was still ticking. I lifted a piece of concrete to expose more of the body and found only a pulpy mass of flesh." His voice becomes choked at this point and he hides his head.

110

After a pause of silence, the first man begins again. "That was quite a place," he says. "At the end of the Oklahoma City mission the town opened their doors. All the rescue workers were loaded onto buses and taken downtown to a renovated part of the city. The stores were open. They told us that could go into any store and get anything we wanted. We could go into any restaurant or bar, drinking as much as we wanted. Our money was no good. Everywhere we went the people thanked us and called us heroes. Personally, I didn't feel like we did a good job. After all, we didn't rescue anyone, all we did was recover remains."

"But that's just as important a part of the mission," says one of the group leaders. "It is just as important as the rescue. It gives the loved ones closure. Those remains represent something to the living. We must have something to bury with our feelings of loss." Suddenly I realize how horrible it must be for all the people in New York City searching for missing loved ones. Not knowing is far more terrible than knowing.

"I found some hands on the roof of one of the buildings downtown," says another man, shifting the conversation to the World Trade Center Disaster. "Where the planes struck the towers, a bunch of body parts were found on the rooftops in the southeast direction. It was the first place we looked, hoping to find airplane parts but finding only body parts."

I am curious about the job they do. "How do you guys do this kind of work? What's it like?" I ask.

The explanation I receive reminds me of hunting for seashells on the beach. "You walk around in a pattern over the debris and scan with your eyes. Suddenly you spot something, a thumb, a piece of clothing, a shoe. Then you start clearing the area around it hoping that it's attached to something, something alive if you're lucky."

"The dogs help," says another man. Some of the dogs are so well trained, almost a part of their master. Together they are a true team. One day I saw a man walking a small dog that could smell remains. The dog carried his leash in his mouth while it was still attached to his collar. He listened to signals from the master.

Short whistles bring him back to the master's side. "The dogs cover a much wider area than we can," he continues. "They bark when they find something, or they get excited. It's almost like they have as much respect for the dead as we do. Mostly, I guess they are quiet animals."

"Like their masters," adds someone.

"Only while they're working," adds another, trying to lighten the mood. "Get us in a bar and we can't shut up."

There is laughter, followed by silence. "I know I'm not going to talk much after this," says someone.

"Me too," I add.

"But that's the wrong thing to do," says one of the group leaders. "That's why we have these sessions," he adds. "We need to talk about it. Don't hold back. Don't keep it inside. That does more harm than good."

There is another pause before someone else begins. "Me and another guy, we found the security tapes in the rubble under the World Trade Center. He knew right where to look. It was a room deep down in the basement. The security guard in the tower was his friend. The guy with me wanted to get those security tapes and review them in hopes of finding out where the people went. He told me later that during the last moments of the disaster his friend had pressed the button that turned the tapes on wide-angle scan mode. I can only imagine what that job must have been like, to watch the faces of terror as the security cameras click from scene to scene, from stairwell, to hallway, to entrance, cycling through horrors I can't begin to imagine."

"Wonder what that guy would have to tell us today," says one of the hardened men on the team. "Geez, I wouldn't have wanted his job."

"As if your job is any easier," I comment. It's all nasty work, from me making maps to being out in the rubble. It's all nasty work.

"His friend, the security guard, is still missing," says the man.

It is strange feeling talking to these men, sharing their thoughts. It is my turn to share. "I grew up in the New York City area," I begin. "Over in Jersey City, where the Holland tunnel comes out and where the Statue of Liberty has her back to us." Some laugh. "I was at the World Trade Center less than six months ago staying at that collapsed hotel that was between the towers. I was here at the FEMA Region II headquarters for training. I can't get the image out of my mind of all the people going to work in the morning. There was a bagel shop right outside of Tower One in the mall. I stopped there in the morning to get a bagel and something to drink while I watched the people pouring out of the subway, turning to go through the doors of Tower One and into the elevators.

"Where have all these people gone?" I ask. No one answers.

"I would leave this shop afterwards and see more people pouring out of other subway exits, all going into the towers and getting into elevators.

"Where are all these people today?" Nobody answers me again. "I can't stop thinking about them. I have seen the signs everywhere in town. I have seen them making copies at Kinkos. In front of the DFO, running from pier 92 to pier 90 is a long plywood wall posted with pictures of them. The missing.

"At Ground Zero, the buildings and the light posts and the barricades. The store windows, the plywood coverings, the debris dumpsters, all are full of small, posted signs. There is even an area called the wall of prayers. When you stop to look at the pictures, the people are smiling. They are photos of them with their pets or with another loved one. I have not seen one sad face in all the signs. Of course nobody frowns when they have their picture taken, but the pictures appear far too cheerful for the occasion."

"They're gone," says someone. "All smoke and ash. Don't worry about them, may they rest in peace."

I go back to work. I am having trouble staying focused and cutting a CD for one of the firemen who is going home. I am printing out some pictures for them to take. Evening briefing

113

comes. Afterwards we have a meeting where Greg welcomes all the new people. We have a short GIS meeting afterwards. We already decided on some standards, but I keep the meeting short. For the sake of the newcomers I tell the guys not to worry about making the map perfect, it will be corrected in the next publication. There is still a chance that someone is alive. The search and rescue teams have told us that if someone at least has water there's a chance for them to be found alive. These were office buildings. They have water coolers and there were bathrooms. People kept drinks at their desks, maybe they had bottled water. There's a chance.

The quality and types of maps have been going up. The Minnesota boys have registered the aerial photos. They can tell the size of the debris pile using the polygon method I described earlier. It spans nearly thirty acres. They have superimposed the lower levels of the subways on some maps. They can layer in the mall so

people know approximately where the stores once where. The base picture with the pile of debris superimposed on the map of the mall helps a lot. Someone suggests labeling some of the features that the rescue workers have named like the fingers and the widow maker and the potato chip.

Greg is getting ready to go down to Ground Zero again. It is nighttime and he asks if I want to go. I've had enough of it. I'm shook up, staring at the computer screen. He puts his hand on my shoulder and tells me that I have a good heart. He tells me that I did not kill those people. I tried to help them. It is not the last time I will hear that phrase.

Rick is excited. He hasn't been down to Ground Zero yet, so he grabs his camera and suits up. As he is getting ready to leave, there is a commotion at the front door. Celebrities have come to visit us and cheer us up, kind of like a USO tour during wartime. Dad got Bob Hope, we get Chevy Chase. Ronnie Howard is with him, talking at random to the search and rescue teams. Chevy is cutting up, Ronnie is just smiling goofy- like. He is asking them questions about their jobs. The rescue workers, on the other hand, are asking him questions about Backdraft, which appears to be their favorite movie. I get the impression that Ronnie is doing research for his next film.

Rick gets their autographs and also someone else he doesn't even know, just some guy who happens to be hanging around with them. Several days later he finds out that this guy was some news reporter. Everyone is celebrity crazed for the moment. I see Rick off, the team is ready to move out. A supervisor shows up and tells me not to worry, that I can go back to GIS. He says that he will make sure that the actors come back this way and talk to us after they are through with Search and Rescue. I go back to work.

It's quiet in GIS. Brandon, the forest service guy, is the only one who stayed behind in GIS with me. He's going through pictures and cataloging them. These are the pictures that he takes every day when he goes down to Ground Zero. The same view in the same direction from the same spot at approximately the same time of day. The pictures help photo document the progress.

115

A group of people wander into GIS. They are nosing around for a few moments when I finally get up and ask them if there is something I can do for them.

"We're the actors," one of them says. "We've come to visit you."

I don't recognize him or the others, my wife is the Hollywood insider, not I. I'm not much of a television watcher, more of a computer monitor watcher. They introduce themselves. One of them is Peter Gabriel, another is one of the Baldwin boys, another is Fisher Stevens.

Since I don't know these actors I talk to them as I would anyone else. I show them some of the maps and explain what we do in GIS, my standard tour for visitors. One of the actors is studying one of the aerial photos. He points to a building a few blocks away from the Trade Center. "My girlfriend lives in a terrace apartment here," he says. "She phoned me from there on the morning of September 11 to tell me that the building was collapsing. I kept telling her to get out of there, screaming at her to leave, but she stayed there watching, talking to me on the phone the whole time and describing it."

"That must have been a horrible sight," I say.

"Since that, she has left her apartment. It had a beautiful patio that overlooked one of Manhattan's most stunning views. Now the smoke and the smell have changed that. It's a real mess down there," he says. "We went back to her apartment to get some of her things." His eyes go empty and he looks down at the floor. He shakes his head and repeats himself. "It's a real mess down there."

The actors move on. I offer them a map and a picture. I get their autographs on one of my base of operation maps because it has the date on the top. Brandon and I go back to work and GIS is once again quiet. Brandon peeks from behind his computer occasionally, pointing at other actors that are wandering around. He indicates someone over by the operations table, telling me that he plays a lawyer on "The Practice." He points to another actor who is on "The West Wing." I'm sorry that I don't watch any of these shows.

Suddenly Brandon spots one of his heroes: Sam Waterston. He tells me this guy's been acting for long time, putting that punk Baldwin kid to shame. To his surprise Sam comes over to GIS. I get him to pose with Brandon while I take a picture.

Sam also signs my BoO map (short for Base of Operations). He thanks us for being there and helping out, then he moves on. Brandon tells me that he wished he had told Sam his comment about being a brilliant actor compared to the Baldwin kid. He wishes he were a little quicker. Truly he is one of Sam's biggest fans.

It has been an exciting night and a long day. Brandon is ready to go home too. Barry, who works the night shift, has come in, and it is after midnight. "It's time to go home," I tell Brandon. "Come on, I'll give you a ride."

On the way home I am driving like a New Yorker. I am having trouble seeing. Something happened to my eyeglasses at ground zero. They haven't been right since. The coating on my lenses interacted with the fumes and permanently fogged them. They are almost like frosted glass. I whip around a corner and scare a pedestrian that I didn't see. He starts arguing, gesticulating and cursing at me. I shrug apologetically and he moves on.

Brandon starts laughing. A week ago New York was meek. I sense that the city is beginning to heal enough to allow the luxury of contention, which I guess is a good thing and the norm around here.

"We must be getting close to recovery," says Brandon.

"What makes you say that?" I ask.

"The animals are out again."

"What do you mean?" he asks.

"In every wildfire we find the safe place where all the animals hole up. You'll find a glen or a valley and there is every animal from the forest. Fox sitting beside deer beside rabbit and hawk, all coexisting together. There comes a nervous time after the fire is out. All bets are suddenly off as the animals slowly move off, merging back into their niches, returning to life as it was before the fire."

I see what he means. The predators are out.

Building Structural Damage Through September 26, 2001

Thursday
September 22

I spend the day tidying up loose ends. It seems like there is so much to do to bring my work to closure. It would be an impossible task if I really sat down and thought about it, but some strange sense of duty drives me in this matter. I think this is true of all FEMA people. Every time I participate in an operation, there is always more work than time. The urgency and timeliness of every task make it a difficult and stressful environment. About the time you begin to feel caught up, you get the FEMA farewell. Somebody comes up and says, "You did a good job. Bye," and you are home before you know it. I don't like to stay out too long, a standard FEMA deployment is 21 days. There are some who will

119

try to stay until the last piece of paper has been signed and filed away. Personally, I don't know it's right to try to make a living off of disasters, but somebody has to do the work. Full time FEMA employees are different. They spend a lot of between time on mitigation, disaster preparedness, and training missions. Someone needs to be doing that, reviewing the events and improving our ability to respond. Also there is a phenomenal amount of paperwork mandated by the government and by regulations that result from a disaster. There are people who help during the Response phase and there are those who specialize in Recovery. The timing and the need for replacements are critical. Some show up three to four weeks into the disaster. They set up bureaucratic processes, paperwork and training mandates. They tighten budgets and put an end to new purchases. These people are an essential part of the operation, just as important as the high stress type A's who are first on the scene as part of the initial response.

One time I was at a disaster where office space was a premium. There was physically not enough room in the building for the amount of people that had to squeeze in. Folks were complaining about all manner of things. One of the guys in charge said if anyone had complaints, he would talk to them. He was an understanding guy. Someone went to him complaining that their telephone was on the wrong side of their computer. Another complained that they didn't have a chair. Another complained about declining per diem. He sent them all home. Sometimes people forget why they're here. It's not about our comfort, it's about comforting the victims.

Having lived through a catastrophic hurricane and seeing it through the eyes of the victims, I know what the priorities are. FEMA recruits a lot of help from victims that went through disasters. They sign on as local hires, kind of like a trial period, and if they find the work suitable they can apply to become Disaster Assistance Employees, a title given to "Full Time" temporary help. Like myself, DAE's are on call and ready for action when they are needed. Not surviving a disaster first hand might be compared to being a publisher without ever having read a book or visiting a library. Something I like about former FEMA Director James Lee Witt: he was in a tornado and he lost his house. He suffered and he learned what effect a disaster can have on an individual.

The hurricane was scary to me. Picture windows turned into flying glass that circled the room like bees until the roof was ripped off, sucking the glass out along with a ten foot oak table that was never seen again. The rain fell sideways. I looked up into the sky, thinking how it looked just like a high-speed film clip. The sound, more like a roar than a howl, assaults your ear drums until they pop, leading you to wonder if it is the drop in air pressure or the sheer force of the wind that is the cause.

Adrenaline pumped, exploding me into action after the first clash. I gained superhuman strength that night. I emptied the closet, tossing a heavy roll-away bed aside like it was a pillow, scattering toys and clothing to make room for a mattress. That is where I spent the night with my family. I lived through a tornado on a boat once before that. The tornado was over in a matter of minutes. The hurricane went on forever. The floor shook. I heard the classic freight train sound and watched nearby floorboards pry themselves up. I never heard the sound of the remaining roof separate from the house, all I heard was the wind. When the wind stopped, the rain fell down instead of sideways. Everything got wet and miserable. Small gusts that sounded like the slightest whoosh brought on fits of anxiety. Flood victims experience the same thing during that first hard rain after the disaster.

In the days that followed it was like a descent into Maslov's hierarchy of needs. Self-actualization was far from my mind; it was all about shelter, food, water, and the basics. Days passed before we reached the level of thinking about security. We had a hidden flare gun in case of a problem. It was a post apocalyptic world in which everything had changed. There were lines in town for all the basic commodities: ice, gas, food and water. ATM machines do not work without electricity and with no phones or telecommunications, credit cards are also useless. Cash is king. Even after we found an apartment to rent, we did not have power until ten weeks later.

The vegetation had been stripped of leaves as easily as we had been stripped of all our material possessions.

The mind does not function the same following a disaster. Stress can override normal functions. In the aftermath of the hurricane I saw looting, riots, racial snobbery, but I also saw the opposite: community support, group prayer, and the total erasure of prejudice. "Thank God for life," was the catch phrase, the greeting of the day. I think that a disaster is God's way of testing you. At the very least you will find out what you're made of. You either rise to the occasion or you crumble under forces beyond your ken. Having been in a disaster, I have a special appreciation for the victims, and I owe FEMA a lot. They were there when I needed them. My service is a way of returning that sense of duty and responsibility, of being there when others are in need. It has meaning for me and it brings meaning to my life.

The good thing about it all is that there are a lot of people in FEMA like me. Many of us have been victims of natural disasters. We came looking for help and found ourselves helping instead. I heard the phrase once that when a man's house is on fire you pitch in and help him out, you don't offer to sell him lumber at twice the price so he can rebuild.

Lots of people are going home. Urban search and rescue teams usually have a two-week deployment. Considering the nature of their work, that is almost too long. Also, after two weeks the chance of finding someone alive is pretty slim. But at that point it becomes a recovery operation, which means the focus is on recovering remains. Recovery is just as important as rescue. Fresh teams are brought in, the replacements are necessary and needed. Somehow, in the mindset of the rescue worker, it seems like failure. Searching is a race against death, a race with slim odds to win, with the ultimate cost of self-esteem if you lose.

The rescue dogs know that. When they work all day with no results, they experience anxiety and depression. Out behind the Javitz Center, Search and Rescue has set up a miniature course where they take the dogs at the end of the day. They run the course and find something, get their treat or reward along with the satisfaction and feeling of success, even if it is fake and manufactured. In the end, they are happy and ready to search again on the next day. If only the humans were as lucky.

I discover this as I continue to talk throughout the day to all of the people involved in this operation. Again the phrase comes up, "You did not kill these people." To me the phrase triggers acceptance, it is a statement of fact, a truth, yet there remains a feeling of failure. These feelings are natural they say. You never feel like you can do enough. We have all been working long hours and very hard. Some of these feelings are just a part of the general exhaustion. Others are rooted in the psychological ramifications of what we've experienced and what we know about the details of this operation.

Last night I had a dream. I was at my computer. I had no hands and was tapping the keys with stumps that ended at my wrists. I was working on a map or writing something. I felt someone touch my hand, even though I did not have hands. They had been severed. I realized then it was a rescue worker picking it up and placing it in a plastic bag. I was screaming at him to find the other one, telling him that they come in sets of two, but he did not find it. I know dreams like this are stress induced, but it does not lessen their impact.

What is the purpose of these sessions, this talking, the sharing? The purpose of the debriefing is to help us get it all out, to deal with it, and to leave it behind. FEMA has some standard pamphlets that they give us. They are always written in terms of leaving the disaster. They tell us that when we go home, there may be people who are not interested in the disaster or in what happened to us. We hear that we will be expected to go back to normal rules, to be reintegrated into our families.

Here is a common story. We work all day at a disaster, then at night we often go to restaurants to eat. It's fun for while, but after weeks of restaurant food people begin to crave a normal home cooked meal. But as soon as you get home the first thing your spouse wants to do is go out to dinner with you. Such is the irony of life.

But I am going home tomorrow. I am so detached from the work that I don't even attend the nightly GIS meeting. Instead I stay at my computer and try to wrap up what I am doing. I say goodbye to all the people that I have worked with. I am not the only one going home. I make sure a few personal things that I want to accomplish get done. For one thing, the CD full of pictures. I am finally ready to relinquish my computer.

We leave work early that night. By early I mean 10:00. There are plans to meet at Rosie O'Grady's tonight for one final get together. This time Stavros is not excused from attending. The pub is crowded. People are in a good mood, trying to escape the confines of the tragedy outside. Stavros orders some hors 'd oeuvres and in no time we receive the largest plate of appetizers that I've ever seen. Once again New Yorkers make us feel welcome.

I find myself sitting next to a guy who was one of the fire marshals on a floor of the World Trade Center. It was one of the lower floors, which is why he is alive and here to tell his story. "Everyone on my floor made it out," he announces proudly. "For years this job was really nothing but filling out paperwork, checking fire extinguishers to make sure they were filled, looking at sprinkler systems and smoke alarms, and dealing with regular visits and inspections from the local fire department. And then one day you go to work and this happens."

Another man is a textbook salesman. One of his clients was in the World Trade Center. He was planning a visit to the building that day. He is an old man, an old world salesman who takes a personal interest in his clients. As he talks, it soon becomes obvious that he misses his friends.

Someone has bought me a beer. I am not much of a drinker these days but I have a few sips out of courtesy, enjoying the cold against my palate. The bartender tells me a man named Patrick bought it for me. He nods and smiles. I go over and talk to him. He knew a lot of people who worked there. He seemed to be drinking

124

a lot to try to forget what has happened. I think it's a lost cause. This is something that will be hard to forget. Still, I tap my glass to his and down the icy liquid with a smile and a sincere "Thank you."

Some more of the guys from work show up. They come to say goodbye to me and tell me how much they've enjoyed working with me. Two beautiful women come into the bar. Greg and Stavros are talking and I hear one of them make a crack about how they look high maintenance. The women stop and nuzzle in at the bar on the other side of Greg and within minutes he's talking to them. He is very gregarious and very much enjoys the company of people. Stavros is getting tired. He is leaving in the morning too. I see an opportunity (more an excuse) to get back to the hotel and pack tonight so I can get out of the city early tomorrow. I have had enough of this traffic.

Stavros says that his wife wants him to bring her back a souvenir, one of those T-shirts that say "I ♥ New York". We spot a couple of New York's finest standing on a street corner and ask them if there are any souvenir shops open. It is about 1:00 in the morning in Times Square, but they point to a little spot a block away tell us to give it a try.

Sure enough it's open. Stavros is able to find one those T-shirts that his wife wants. The lady behind the counter sees his FEMA badge and charges him two dollars for the shirt. Now that he has completed this final task he too is ready to go home. We agree to meet the next morning at nine, where I will give him the ride to the convention center and then check out in the morning.

Once in the hotel room, I spent most of my last night packing, a little too excited to go sleep. Tonight I dream of home, free from another disaster-induced nightmare.

Friday
September 21

My last day in New York.

I am up early. The phone rings about 7:30 in the morning. It is Stavros wondering if I am awake. He wants to know if I would like to get out of here sooner. He is taking a plane out of Newark and has a rental car to return. He is worried about traffic. I have been up for an hour and I am ready to go. We meet in fifteen minutes at the front desk and are on the road in less than a half an hour.

I park outside and go into the Convention Center for the last time. I say my goodbyes again. His rental car is there in a secure lot, free of a forty five dollar a night charge.

"What time did you finally pack it in last night?" I ask Greg, surprised to see him up so early.

"I don't know," he says. "Pretty late."

"How long did you spend talking to those women?"

"You know they overheard us saying they were high maintenance. That's why they came over and sat down at the bar, just to prove they weren't." Greg has a sly grin and I know he had a good time talking to them.

"Yeah, yeah," I say. "Listen, I want to get out of here and hit the road. Just want to tell you how much I enjoyed working with you."

"Drive safely," he says. "I enjoyed working with you too. You have a big heart."

"You too," I say. "I enjoyed hearing about your experiences in Oklahoma City. I underestimated you the first time I met you."

"What'd you think," he asks. "Did you think I was an asshole?"

I am caught off guard by the question. It tells me that fundamentally he must have doubts about himself. All people in command or in positions have these doubts, at least the good ones do. They act hard and stern, saying things they sometimes regret.

126

He is definitely a different person than the one I met 10 days ago, but it is natural for people to keep their guard up when they first meet. He is demanding because he is a fire chief and is used to being in command during an emergency situation. He has not stopped working hard for one minute. After a pause I answer "Yes," and smile kinda goofy. "You're an asshole." That big heart of mine is stuck in my throat. To answer any other way would have resulted in an emotional scene, and we all know guys don't do that sort of thing. I look forward to working with him again in the future.

There are many quick goodbyes and I am anxious to leave. I cut it short, gather the last of my things, and head over to Pier 90 where I must fill out a stack of paperwork and obtain an autograph book full of signatures to finalize my release. And you thought checking in was bad.

Traffic is still a nightmare in the city. Around Pier 90, it is crowded with pedestrians, cars, bicycles, and trucks. Everything is stop-and-go. I look around and notice the signs again, the posters looking for missing loved ones. Maybe they wandered up here in shock after the tragedy. Maybe they're a block away in an alley hanging around with some homeless guys. All 10,000 of them.

In the stalled traffic I notice a plywood wall that runs for blocks along the west side of the highway. It is decorated with letters and posters of the missing. Occasionally there is a picture drawn by a school kid but mostly it is the missing. Like the Vietnam War Memorial it has an air of tragedy, a sadness transcended only by a deadening sense of loss. This is not the world of two weeks ago.

There are several checkpoints to go through. Police inspect the car and check my badge. Further down near the parking lot my trunk is opened and my luggage is inspected. Overhead I see two military helicopters circling. Next to the pier I see the hospital ship *Comfort*. Near the stern is a large gun behind sandbags. There is a third checkpoint going into the FEMA office on the pier where my credentials are once again checked.

I report in at Information and Planning. This is where I would probably be if I had never gone forward to work with Search and Rescue. The place looks clean compared to the convention center. Everything is bright and white. There is a big picture window looking north over the water out at the *Comfort*. No rats. Don't think I ever mentioned seeing rats every night at the convention center. They would move along the exposed metal girders that run horizontal about ten feet off the floor. My biggest worry was that they would chew on the network cables and we would lose connectivity. No rats here, though. The convention center roof also leaked. We had to cover the equipment with plastic during a heavy rain. Designed by I.M. Pei, it has lots of weird angles and odd shaped windows which always tend to leak in these types of buildings. I used to work construction in a former life. I learned that if you use standard building materials you not only save money but you also avoid many of these problems.

Paul, the Section Chief of Information and Planning, is his usual self. This man stays calm in a storm and manages to have an uplifting comment at every turn. He is the one responsible for ordering the special printers that print on indestructible paper. This is my second time working with him. I am looking forward to working with him again at some future operation. I hear his famous catch phrase for the first time in this disaster as he tells me "You did a yeoman's job."

I meet another fellow I had worked with yet never met. Franklin was the third person on the road trip with Rob and Barry from the west coast to New York via D.C. He has helped me from headquarters numerous times, providing mapping and analysis support to us bums in the field who lack the resources of giant computers and unlimited datasets. I could sacrifice a workstation for a day and let it crank away trying to match 100,000 addresses with street segments on a map, or I could email the Excel file to Franklin and have a ready to use data layer back in an hour.

I promise him that his children will play with mine when this is all over. I'm not far from D.C. so it's a promise that will be easy to keep.

Processing my paperwork goes fairly rapidly. I must be evaluated, have my final timesheet signed, go through travel to have my reimbursement paperwork processed, and obtain release signatures from accountable property signifying that I have returned all Government materials checked out in my name. I have never been here let alone used anything from this facility, but I still must obtain signatures and go through the motions. There is also a network administrator's signature to obtain so they can delete any temporary logins that I might have been assigned, and a telecommunications officer to visit so he can update the phone book and reassign the telephone extension. There's always a waiting list for phones. I can understand why many people bring and use their own.

I'm free! The last piece of paper is signed and I have my copies in case they get lost. As a final measure, I wait to talk to a counselor for an exit interview.

It is post cathartic, but I am feeling sad and emotional. The counselor's name is Barbara. She wears a khaki army uniform and has a name tag that identifies her as belonging to the National Institute of Mental Health. We talk for a while. I tell her about seeing all the posters on my way over here, that I can't stop thinking about all the missing people. I tell her I refuse to believe the statistics even though I have a paper that says only 5,000 are missing. I am convinced someone is lying. I tell her about some of the things I have experienced. At one point I lose it and get watery. She has no tissues and offers me a KimWipe instead. KimWipes are laboratory tissues. I must be having an industrial strength cry.

"It's okay to remember these things," she says. "You will remember everything for some time. You will remember the people you worked with and the experiences you shared with them. You will remember me," she says, smiling. "You will remember the visit to Ground Zero, you will remember details and events that may disturb your sleep and make you prone to outbursts. Are you married?" she asks.

"Yes," I answer.

"How old is your wife?" she asks. I tell her. Barbara asks, "Has been through menopause?"

"Yes," I say. "Still going through it."

She taps my hand. "You tell her I said to treat you like you are menopausal and it will help her relate." I laugh. "Above all, talk to her about it. Get it in the open and begin the healing process. Get it out," she says. "Don't hold back. Get over it."

Again I hear the phrase as she says, "You did not kill those people." I know this but something is broken inside. Why do I feel so responsible? It is because I also feel helpless?

Barbara has a soothing voice. She gives me some papers and pamphlets and points out things to read. They mention feelings and events, things about disasters that I have experienced first hand. There is something called John Wayne Syndrome where rescue workers have this drive to succeed in their mission while trying to remain strong and untouched. We think we are superhuman and do not need to seek help. Movie behavior, larger than life stories glamorized by Hollywood. Normally the result is burnout, something she warns me about. She urges me to use my support group, to let my wife hear all the nasties, to even journal it as I have done here.

I feel better. I have stopped crying and begin to compose myself for the trip home. I notice she has a bracelet on that is only made in St. Croix. She smiles and I find out that she too has been to the Virgin Islands as part of the response to Hurricane Marilyn. My wife has a bracelet just like it.

I am ready to go home. I feel renewed in a way, like Barbara took upon herself the burden of my tears. I disagree with what she said, though, I do not want to bring all that excess baggage home with me. But I will follow her advice and talk about it when I feel the need.

Getting out of the city is a nightmare. Traffic is bumper-to-bumper leaving through the Lincoln Tunnel. I feel relieved when I finally hit the Jersey Turnpike and begin speeding away from everything. In Pennsylvania I pass a tanker overturned on the opposite side of the highway. I think of the policeman I worked with in my early days at the convention center, of how he must be back at his normal job, glad to be responding to similar events instead of stuck answering a phone. I am also returning to my normal life as well. I have 300 miles to get my thoughts in order and prepare for the reintegration with my family. Each mile pulls me farther away from New York and everything going on there. Each mile draws me closer to home.

Bonnie calls when I am near. She orders a pizza and tells me to pick it up on my way home. I pull in the driveway and she tells my son to go outside and help the pizza guy. She told him that I wasn't coming home until tomorrow. I hear him complaining about why he has to help the pizza guy, but when he sees me his face lights up. I am nearly knocked down by the speeding hug I receive. I pick him up, carry him through the front door where I see a poster board drawing of a dinosaur in front of an American Flag. It says "Welcome Home Dad."

That was the moment it was all over for me. I thank Barbara, beginning to cry for joy instead of sadness. Yes, I will remember, and I will get over this.

I am home.

PART II

RECOVERY

Saturday
September 22

I go to my son's soccer game today. It feels so real to see the green grass, the bright colors of the uniforms, the crisp, blue sky overhead. I realize that everything had been shades of gray in New York City. The city is normally gray with gray building-lined canyons and gray concrete underneath. When I did go outside, it was to visit Ground Zero where the smoke was gray, the sky was gray, the debris was gray, and even people's faces were gray. Now life seems so much more real, I still cannot believe that I was there.

Bonnie has arranged for the local news media to interview me and talk about my experience. People are curious, and I was told to talk about it. I agree to the interview. They are coming to the soccer game and will interview me there.

The questions are simple and I answer them easily. I talk about the priest I met, about the sheer size of the site. I show them a picture that I have, one of the aerial images of the site from above. I mention statistics, the 29 acres or more of debris, the height of the pile, the hard work we did. I mention the President's visit, the celebrities, and the endless support we received from businesses, the public, and the numerous government agencies involved. They interview Bonnie as well. She tells them she thinks of me as a hero, risking my life to be there to help. That much may be true, but I do not feel like a hero. To me, all the real heroes are buried under the debris: firemen and policemen who risked life and limb and lost. The ultimate sacrifice. Many of the men and women I worked with at the convention center felt the same way. Most of the policemen and firemen who lost their friends and kindred officers in the disaster all feel the same way.

I get to hear some of it from her perspective. She tells them about the quick calls I made to say, "I love you. Gotta go." She talks about the worry she has endured. The general worry about the world situation and what evil plots may now be hatching in Afghanistan or even in hidden corners of our own great nation. She talks about the support she has received from friends and co-workers who know where I have been and what I was doing. People respect FEMA and the job that it entails.

I miss most of the soccer game because of the interview. It doesn't matter. I know there will be other games, other days that smell as sweet and are just as colorful. A midst this fleeting moment of joy, I realize what I must do next. I have a funeral to attend in Charlottesville.

The drive is uneventful. As promised, my entire family is gathered at my Uncle's house. It is a solemn event but I am glad to see everyone. My Uncle's house is full yet it feels empty. I am wondering where my feelings are. I am not sad. Perhaps it is because I had made peace with him when I saw him last. Closure for me begins with the living. A funeral is almost too late. It seems again that I have cried more for the loss of life at the World Trade Center disaster than for the death of my own uncle.

We begin to organize and form the funeral procession. My son wants to ride in the limousine. This is his first funeral and everyone understands and so they grant a child his wish.

I am all right until I reach the funeral home. Outside I realize where I am and why I am here and the tears begin. I feel the grief and loss all at once. I relate it to what I have been going through, thinking about how it must be for the loved ones in New York. I think of all those signs advertising the missing. At least I know where my uncle is. I realize how important closure is to the living.

I go inside. I am introduced to a child that my Uncle had, a cousin that I never knew about. I remember meeting her mother once, and she reminds me of going to the Rocky Horror Picture Show with her years ago when I lived in Florida. I like her. I wonder what other things I don't know about my uncle. Everyone is entitled to their secrets.

My Uncle was cremated. Ashes. Now I begin crying over ashes as I think of the thousands that were cremated in the collapse of the towers.

The room is hot. People are fanning themselves with paper. It reminds me of a stereotyped southern funeral. My son sits up front with his grandmother. The ceremony is simple. People stand and say something about my Uncle. They tell little vignettes and anecdotes about him. My Uncle was into Alcoholics Anonymous, twenty years of sobriety. There are a lot of people from the local group who have great things to say about him. His life has touched many people and it has been full. One cannot ask for anything greater. Even my son gets up and says something about Uncle Joe. My family is surprised and proud of him for saying something. The heat is unbearable but the testimonials go on, a tribute to my Uncle. His daughter gets up and reads some emailed notes sent by people who could not attend.

Afterwards we return to the house for a wake. Relatives are curious about what I went through in New York and I answer many questions. They mostly want to know what it was like to meet the President. I am happy to answer such questions. I am tired of being in the company of death.

There are the usual arguments of who gets what. These things are silly to me. I already carry the best part of my Uncle in my heart, all else is material and superficial. He gave me a wonderful book of his poems that he compiled during his last days. They are deeply personal and reveal things about him I did not suspect. He was a very spiritual person, a Harvard graduate, and a humanitarian. The arguments seem petty and people try to get me to take sides. I make a promise to myself to give it all away before I die and settle any posthumous debate over who gets what.

A neighbor is helping with the wake. She goes around cleaning and picking up after people. This is a southern tradition, helping a neighbor when there is a death in the family is part of community ties. I find out later that she has been more than a neighbor and done a lot. Along with my mother, she cared for my Uncle during his darkest hours.

The time for goodbyes comes all too soon. Members of my immediate family are staying at my house so we gather up and caravan back to my house several hours away. The rest of the day is joyful despite the tragedy, more like a family reunion than a funeral.

Monday
September 24

I have decided to rest today. The events of the weekend, the endless driving, the funeral, and a house full of relatives have left me exhausted. Bonnie spends the morning with me. It is raining outside and I sit on my covered deck listening to the drops fall heavy upon the Earth. It brings back a memory of how we feared the rain in New York. It compacted the debris and made the crushed concrete rubble harden so that a shovel became useless. I remember Greg telling me that it would be like this, that something would trigger the memories, that the experience would be with me the rest of my life.

I remember Barbara telling me that it is good to get it out, that it is part of the healing process. I tell myself that I had forgotten about recovering bodies in Rio Piedras and that I will forget about this too. Maybe forget is not the right word. Let me say that it might be easier to remember this horrid past, that emotions will not surface as easily, and that some sense of closure will put it all in perspective.

I know that I am healing.

Tuesday
September 25

My first day back on the job. I learn that Management told my supervisor to dump me and replace me after I had left for New York City. He refused, arguing that the company had announced that employees who needed to serve their country in this trying time would be granted the privilege of going and coming. He wondered why that courtesy did not extend to contractors as well. He also has faith in my abilities to do the job. In one moment I feel betrayed by the company, yet my loyalty to my supervisor has increased. I have just returned from defending the honor of Corporate America after a vicious attack against Wall Street and this is my reward. It only drives home the reason why I do not work full time for a large corporation. Some of them have no respect for individual life. Support often comes from coworkers and not from the company. They expect loyalty but offer none in return. I have lived through my share of down-sizings and layoffs. Still it makes me wonder.

I slide easily back into the routine, focusing on work that does not revolve around death and destruction. A few people are curious and I share my experiences with them. It has become easier to talk about it and to show them the pictures that I have brought back with me.

That night I go to a PTA meeting at my son's school. I look forward to doing something normal, meeting my son's teacher and listening to the mundane chatter that comprises the agenda. At an opening ceremony in the school auditorium, Cub Scouts advance and place the colors in flag holders and I say the pledge of allegiance with renewed vigor. Then there is a moment of silence for the victims of the terrorist attack against the World Trade Center. My expression changes from joyful anticipation to sudden emptiness. I stare down at the floor, the smile evaporated from my face. The ghosts of 5,000 people are still with me.

Afterwards, a woman stops me in the hall and says that she saw me on television. She is thankful that someone from our town went up there to help. I tell her I am fortunate to have a job with FEMA. It is in my nature to help, but again I do not feel like the hero she is praising me as. Again I think, the real heroes are buried in the rubble. I am not worthy to walk away unscathed. I think about that and I realize that I am not unscathed. The memory of what I have been through is burned in my consciousness. Sadness returns too easily and too quickly.

I visit my son's teacher. "Thanks for sending those maps to school. I was just teaching them about the scale bar the other day," he says, pointing to the scale bar on the map.

I look at the map but still have no appreciation for the size of the destruction. "I can't believe that the towers were on 14 acres alone. The debris pile is 30 acres."

"The kids were full of questions that your son couldn't answer," he says. "I was wondering if you would come in and talk to them."

Suddenly I hear Barbara in the back of mind, telling me that it is good to talk about it, to pull it out from the depths of my experience to a place where I can see it and deal with it.

It is part of healing.

Wednesday
September 26

Business as usual. I have not thought about the disaster all day. I am distracted, almost sick of hearing about it. I watch stories of heroes on television, a doctor who teamed with two carpenters to help set up a triage unit in the Staten Island Ferry terminal. The story has a sad ending. They prepared a field hospital to help thousands but only a trickle of people came.

Then there was a port authority cop who was helping evacuate people from the mall under the towers. He is on television talking about it. He was moving everyone along when the first tower collapsed. "There was a noise and it kept getting louder and louder. Suddenly the ceiling fell in. The rush of air blew me down the hallway of the mall and slammed me against a wall. It was dark then, the darkest night you can imagine. I crawled through the rubble and made it out."

"Come on," says a friend. "Tell them the story. He didn't just crawl through the rubble, he pulled a bunch of people out of there with him. This guy's a hero."

"I'm not a hero," he says.

"Yes you are. Go ahead and tell them."

He starts reluctantly. "I heard voices, people yelling. I yelled back. I told them I had a flashlight. In that darkness, it was so dark that the flashlight was almost useless. I said if you can hear me, come to my voice. If there's anyone next to you grab them and bring them along. Grab an arm, grab a shirt and come this way. We all crawled out of there holding on to each other. I led them down a level into the subway then we went over and up to safety."

"See, he's a real hero."

There are more stories, except they are mixed, one of hope and bravery, one of tragedy.

I walk away and cry again. Bonnie has seen me like this enough. It's not fair to her. I tell myself I will not cry today, but it is hard when I am also writing about it. This memoir is important to me. It represents closure.

The tears come.

Yes, I am continuing to heal.

Friday
September 27

I start my day by visiting my son's class. I begin by telling them what FEMA is and what they do. We respond to disasters. I name the four most common disasters: hurricane, flood, earthquake, and tornado. There have been other variants: ice storms, droughts, even the West Nile Virus outbreak in New York and New Jersey during the summer of 2000 which was a medical disaster. But this disaster is something different. This one is man made.

I tell them how I got into FEMA, talking about the hurricane that Bonnie, my son, and I were in. When Marilyn hit in 1995 we were in St. Thomas. The storm spawned tornadoes that destroyed a whole row of houses in the area of the island in which we lived. We spent the night in the closet praying not for salvation but for mercy: let us all go at once so the living that remain do not suffer alone. Life was God's judgment that day, but the destruction of the house was catastrophic.

I show the kids pictures of my son happily driving his tricycle through the debris and they laugh. I tell them that as I cleaned up the mess, I would find things and he would cheer me up. "Look, Daddy, this plastic dinosaur is okay." I tell them that kids are resilient and they bounce back quickly. It is their advantage. I point out the look on Bonnie's face in the picture. I have seen that look a lot lately, the face of disaster. It was on the firemen and the rescue workers returning from Ground Zero. I have seen it in flood victims, in hurricane survivors, and in others who have seen death and catastrophic destruction close at hand.

I realize I have been avoiding the subject. The kids want to know in particular about the World Trade Center disaster. I choose my words carefully. I use "remains" instead of dead bodies, I never mention body parts or morgues, I avoid talking about the casualties and instead focus on debris and damage, anything but people. I tell them what a good job the City of New York Fire Department and the Police Department are doing. I praise the Mayor and the President.

"How about the gold?" one kid asks. "I heard there was a lot of gold in vaults inside the towers. Did they ever find it?"

"I don't know," I answer to the best of my knowledge. "I haven't heard about that, but there were a lot of brokerage houses in the Tower. It's an interesting question. I wonder how they would find it in all that mess."

"I thought the Towers were safe," says another. "How could the planes crash into the towers like that?"

I tell them what engineers told me. "When they designed the towers, they were built to withstand a plane crash. A plane hit the Empire State Building once and it survived. But in this case the specifications changed on jet fuel. It got more potent. The tower probably would have made it through the crash if the jet fuel had not been upgraded and increased in octane. The fire raged until it started to melt the steel. The concrete weakened and the floors fell like a domino effect. Like most of the construction in a crowded city, the building was designed to collapse like that so it wouldn't fall over on the surrounding buildings. Once the floors fell down, the structural steel fell on top. The result was a pile of debris thirteen stories high in places. There was a lot of collateral damage, too." I passed around some pictures I brought with me of the buildings across the street and blocks away. "New York lost 15% of their office space in this disaster."

They want more.

I tell them about the rescue operations. Someone asks about the dogs and I break my code for a minute. "Did you know there are two kinds of rescue dogs, those that sniff for live bodies and those who sniff for dead bodies? You can also see pictures of real rescue dogs on the FEMA website." I show them some printouts I have made of the trading cards available on the public FEMA for kids site. They are pictures of rescue dogs with little stories about them, just like sports heroes. They think it's pretty cool. "The dogs work hard, but get nervous when they don't find anything. They want to do their job because they have been trained to get their reward when they find something. The dogs get hurt in the line of duty, too, but there are veterinarians there to treat them in case that happens." They are fascinated.

I try to wrap things up by telling them not to worry. I know they are afraid of terrorists and of what can happen, but our government is on the job. We are vigilant and painfully aware of our shortcomings in security and in monitoring terrorist activity. I tell them what the President said to me: to pray and to work hard.

They wonder what they can do and I tell them about the cards and pictures that meant so much to the rescue workers. I tell them about my "Welcome Home Dad" sign with a dinosaur in front of an American flag. I show them pictures of the walls and buildings around the Trade Center decorated with messages and drawings that kids made. I tell them about the cards and letters sent to us by the kids in New York. I tell them that they are our future, to study hard and learn everything they can. I mention that some of the smartest people in our nation worked at the World Trade Center, businessmen and women, bankers and computer specialists, consultants and brokers. These are the people who worked hard to get to where they were in life. We will need more people like them. Children are our future.

I end by asking questions and offering rewards to see who was paying attention. Only one can tell me correctly what FEMA stands for. Almost everyone knows the two types of search dogs. I hand out a copy of FEMA for Kids to the winners, the CD produced by the Government for kids. It is basically the FEMA for Kids web site on CD and is a good place to learn more about disasters and disaster preparedness.

They thank me, as does my son's teacher. He says he didn't know all that about FEMA. He quickly launches into his lesson plan, keeping order in the class. I am grateful for the distraction for them. I remember hearing that in the early days of a disaster, keeping children out of school was wrong, that going back to the routine is the best thing to do for them. I gather up my things quickly and leave, stopping at the car to dry my eyes. The memories of all the good people, all the innocent victims, weighs on my heart.

The rest of my day is easy. SQL Server does not hurt and I do not have to bury my face in the monitor to hide my tears from a database of auto parts. Like the children, I find my routine distracting and therapeutic.

Saturday
September 28

My son has gone camping for the weekend. I am home
alone with Bonnie. I work for a while, losing myself in some web
development, then later I get ready for a date. Out alone together,
no kids, a parent's dream!

In the evening we go out to eat at a nice restaurant. A man
sings romantic music while he plays the piano: Sinatra, Dean
Martin, Tony Bennett, that sort of thing. It is very nostalgic and
reminds me of my father. I begin to think about growing up in New
Jersey, which leads me into thoughts about New York. Suddenly I
do not know what has come over me. I am vacant and distracted,
empty of emotion.

Bonnie notices it. It is unfair to her but I am suddenly
depressing company. She can't help but notice. Dinner is ruined.
Despite my efforts to try and cheer up I am sinking into a pile of
debris three hundred miles away.

I engage the piano player in conversation, answering his
call to the audience for requests. He plays *Come Back to Sorrento*
for me, my Grandfather's song. He tells a funny story about
working in an Italian restaurant in Ohio where he and his two
Hungarian band members learned a repertoire of Italian songs just
to survive. I laugh, but it is short lived.

I am quiet the rest of the night. I guess this is what Greg
meant when he said something would trigger it, a smell, maybe a
sound, something I see. How deep does this damage go inside of
me? I vow, like New York City, that I will keep cleaning it up until
it is gone.

Monday
September 30

My friends at a local company have invited me to lunch.
They have seen me on television and want me to share my
experiences with them. Like everyone they are curious. They
choose a restaurant close to where I am currently working, giving
me every convenience. I remember Barbara telling me to talk
about it, that it is good to talk about it. I go, bringing pictures and
samples of maps I have created.

It is different than talking to kids. I can mention the horror
without fear of damaging them. I feel I am taking advantage of
them, burdening them with what I have seen. After talking all
through lunch without being morbid, Lonnie asks the poignant
question: "Are you affected by this?"

"I'll never be the same." I say. "I know I am damaged
goods."

The others at the table know it too. They see it in my eye,
hear it in my voice. The happy go lucky me, the eternal optimist
has gone away. Maybe not gone away, he's just trapped under a
pile of internal debris. I keep trying to dig him out but he is buried
pretty deep. I feel a void inside. Funny, that word meant hope only
a week ago, now it means emptiness.

Outside in my car I fight back the tears again. So this is
what it is like to be menopausal. I sympathize with what my wife
has been going through. I have tried to be there for her and I know
she is there for me, but this is so unfair to her. It is unfair to my
son.

I wake up in the middle of the night and cannot go back to
sleep. I have been working on this memoir and it has given me bad
dreams. Not nightmares, just bad dreams. I am back at work in the
convention center fighting for life. I am at my computer pushing

the print button. Maps come out of the plotter and turn to sheets of rotting flesh, diseased skin with blotches where the map features should be.

It is 5AM. I see the newspaper being delivered outside. I get it and read more about terrorism and about New York. Bush has addressed FEMA in Washington DC telling them what the United States is doing in response to this heinous act. I put the paper down and surf the web. Yahoo has an article on their front page about a large piece of debris being removed with special heavy equipment. Underneath they find a pile of bodies. The tone is set for my day.

I have an 8:00 meeting. I have not been doing much work on the application I am programming. I have fought a cold and the NIMDA computer virus all weekend. Terrorist flu I call it jokingly as I cough my brains out. I wonder how serious Bonnie takes my comments. I think in the back of her mind she is afraid that it could be true. Who knows what will come next? She says something about reaching my incubation period and now I will become the vector to spread their laboratory born disease to the rest of the area. My son does not want to be around me because of the coughing. I begin to wonder myself. Is humor really a mask for fear? Could this really be linked to something I caught at Ground Zero?

After the meeting I am reminded that I have been on television, a local celebrity. Again I begin to talk about it. No holds barred, full disgusting details. The body parts spewn in a cone from the opposite side of the building hit by the plane, fliers with pictures of missing persons, the ghosts of 10,000 people. I have to leave. Nobody asked to hear this. I feel sick myself.

I am driving down the road and I see one of my friends heading towards the coffee shop. I stop and have a cup with him. I enjoy his company, but he must notice that I am distraught. I tell him about some of my experiences and show him the pictures I have with me. He asks if I would mind if he prays for me. He is a minister for a youth group so I welcome his prayers. He lays his hands on me and says something like "Sweet Jesus, we ask that you help your son Bill, who has seen things no one should have to see. Please lighten his burden. He went there to help people, to do good works, for he is a good man…." The prayer goes on and I feel something move inside. Maybe not lighter, but movement nonetheless. Maybe it is the optimist shifting under the internal debris.

My friend gives me his phone number and says to feel free to call him if I need to talk. Somehow he is aware that I must be burdening my wife with all this. He is a kind man, sensitive to humanity, a true man of God. He tells me that he may not be responsive at two in the morning but he will still talk. I laugh.

I thank him and drive off in my car. Alone, I begin to cry again, recalling the words I heard in debriefing. " You did not kill these people, you came here to help them." Suddenly I am saying them out loud, repeating, "I did not kill these people." Even as I write these words my eyes are blurry and my nose runs. I did not kill those people! I tried to help them. It is the truth. Why should these words affect me so much? I think it is because they remind me of the death I have seen. More importantly, it is a mantra I speak, an affirmation that I am blameless. I may be blameless, but nonetheless I feel guilty. What more could I have done? I'm a damned mapmaker, good at what I do. I consistently get high marks everywhere I go in FEMA. I did my best. Why should it not be enough?

Because people still died, despite our best efforts. Despite my best efforts. I remember the fire marshal I met in the bar the last night I was there. He had worked at the World Trade Center and was there when it fell. He was sad, yet proud that he did his job. "Everybody on my floor got out alive," he said. I could tell that was his mantra. Sometimes, no matter how good a job we do, there is a limit. We want to be superhuman. I want each of those firemen and policemen to be superman, standing up from the ruins of the fallen buildings and shaking the rubble free. They are the true heroes, not me. I am not worthy.

Maybe that is what is bothering me. They paid the ultimate sacrifice. We who must remain go on living just the same. In the face of all this it becomes harder to go on living, easier to just give up and die. I resolve to rebuild, starting with myself.

I have become as obsessed as the media. I go to lunch with another contractor. He did not know that I had been in New York City. I volunteer the information, wanting to talk about it again. Barbara is right, I must talk about it. Pull it all out, all the ugliness, and then rebuild in its place.

The contractor tells me about a job he had in college working for a mortuary. After three months he said he found out he did not have the stomach for it. "Thank God I never saw a dead child," he says. "That would have done it for me."

We all have our ghosts, our limitations. That statement tells me he knew what his were. Maybe I am still finding mine. Whatever doesn't kill us makes us stronger, or so they say.

I certainly do not feel strong today.

Wednesday
October 3

I see on the news this morning what was on the Internet already. They are beginning to find bodies as they remove large portions of debris. The description from a construction worker brings back chilling memories. Once a body is found, word spreads quickly. A hush comes over the site and all attention focuses on the squad that is removing the remains. This time it is two firemen. Reverence is the protocol of the moment. I had seen the same thing when I was at Ground Zero. The construction equipment shuts down, all movement stops except for the body removal team. It is

eerie, undeniably disturbing, driving home the point that the priest made: this is a grave.

I did not have any nightmares last night for a change. Instead I was trying to help a depressed Mr. Rogers. He was suicidal and I kept trying to cheer him up and interest him the party we were at. It was a buffet with lots of free snacks, similar to what we would get when we were working the disaster. The message was obvious to Bonnie. The world has changed, no doubt about it.

Today an airplane was hijacked in India. The world keeps on changing.

Thursday
October 4

I had another dream last night. I always dream about Ground Zero these days. Maybe it is because I am working on this book. I often re-live the terror of the victims in my dreams, imagining how awful it must have been. I can forget for a while, becoming absorbed in work, or my son's soccer game, or some other routine. But then I'll hear something on television, or see an article in the paper and it gets triggered all over again. My mind obsesses on it. I suddenly focus on a particular memory of an event in which I was merely a spectator, yet through the magic of my imagination I become a participant, as if I were watching some kind of bizarre new movie that I somehow get trapped in.

In my visions of the airplane I am always mid way back in coach, usually on the left side in a window seat. A lady with big hair sits in front of me, a businessman occupies the aisle seat and there is an empty seat between us. We do not know we are doomed. A terrorist with a bomb strapped to his chest has just told us to keep our seat belts fastened and remain calm. He threatens to slit the stewardess' throat with a box cutter if we do not obey. I look out the window and see New York. "Hey, this is not where we are supposed to be," I announce, standing up. The man with the box cutter glares at me, cold eyes behind a knowing smirk. He nods his head. About that time the whole plane lurches. I tumble forward with no seat belt. Flames engulf us. Some of the passengers are charred instantly, turning into blackened corpses. I fly past them, crashing through the cockpit door and through the front of the plane as if I were invulnerable. An explosion erupts behind me and I hear the screams of office workers.

Suddenly I am with the office workers lying on the floor. Ceiling tiles have fallen everywhere. People lay wounded on the ground begging for help. Others flee towards the stairwells. I pick myself up and begin trying to escape. I sometimes exercise by walking between floors in the stairwells of big buildings, but this is different. I reach down to help the fallen but they are silent, already dead. I place two fingers on someone's jugular vein to feel for a pulse and they transform into a hideous corpse. I run, joining the fleeing masses.

In my dreams I am trapped at that point in an endless stairwell that descends into the very bowels of hell. The walls glow red, and dark shadows from the flames dance upon them. People are screaming and the ground shakes. It is raining debris and we must cover our heads as we flee. I turn every corner of the stairwell, stepping into a mystery, a vast unknown of terror. Around one corner I trip over a pile of writhing bodies, a mass of people sliding down the stairs as if they were dripping out of a bottle of molasses. Around another corner I may walk into a wall of flames, feeling intense pain and heat as I watch my arms turn to blackened stumps. Around still another there is a darkness so black that I must stop and grope my way down the stairs. I often feel bodies beneath my feet as I step on them and make my way down the stairwell.

I escape the horror. It is only a dream for me. I wake up. What about those poor souls I left back there? What about the people who actually lived that terror?

I have talked to other people about these dreams. I am not the only one having these nightmares. People who were not even near New York have these dreams as well as dreams of terrorists. A friend who is a psychologist said that he is doing a booming business since the attacks.

I am up early again, watching the sunrise while I sit in sadness, waiting for the paper boy to deliver another volume of newsprint terror.

Saturday
October 6

    I am scanning with my satellite dish system. I have an old one with a giant dish the size of a small elephant sitting in the yard. It moves on a small motor and points to different satellites. Once you position this beast you can scan the channels for signals. My random scans point me to images of the World Trade Center. I am seeing construction equipment moving debris while a fireman on a ladder sprays a smoking pile.

    I call my family and make them watch. The camera pans after about ten minutes. It zooms away and I get the perspective from the rooftop of a nearby building, looking west I believe. You can see the whole pile, like a giant anthill, activity in all directions. My family suddenly gets an appreciation for what I am saying about the size of it. The camera zooms back in and tightens around a group of men in rescue gear digging intently through a concentrated pile of rubble. I watch this for about ten minutes. What have they found? Is it a body? The camera pans away, now focusing on construction equipment. A front-end loader is scooping and piling rock and debris. In the background a crane is being rigged with a large scrap of metal. I see it lift the twisted trunk of steel and lay it on a long, flatbed truck.

I tell Bonnie I am going to put a tape in. She scoffs at me, branding me as a rubbernecker, a sick kind of disaster junkie. She is right. Why do I want to re-live this when I am trying to forget it? It has been going away, let it fade. Let go.

In my mind I am asking the counselor who debriefed me a pertinent question. Barbara, would you be proud of my progress, or am I going backwards in despair?

Sunday
October 7

Recovery.

I scan the literature that I have thrust aside since I came home. Pamphlets that talk about PTSD: Post Traumatic Stress Disorder. It talks in detail about what I have been experiencing. There is an impact phase, exposure to the disaster. Most people respond appropriately during this phase and react to protect their own lives and the lives of others. This is natural. A range of such behaviors may occur that must be dealt with in the aftermath. Right out of the pamphlet I read:

Several stressors may occur during impact, which may have consequences for the person subsequently:

Threat to life and encounter with death.

Feelings of helplessness and powerlessness.

Loss (e.g. Loved ones, home, possessions)

Dislocation

Feeling responsible, feelings as though could have done more

Inescapable horror, being trapped, being tortured

Human malevolence, particularly difficult to cope with disaster if seen as the result of deliberate human actions.

I have all these symptoms at one time or another. I am suffering from this disorder. Once I can label it as a disease it will be easier for me to deal with its effects. At least this is the way alcoholics deal with it. Now I realize why they put us in a group. We are one big support group, but only for one session. I wonder if I should seek some kind of local help.

No, I say to myself.

I hear Barbara talking. "John Wayne Syndrome" she says. She is right. Rejecting the help is a sign of the sickness. I wonder how my friends from the search and rescue teams are doing. I should have gotten more phone numbers, more email addresses, more points of contact. I did not recognize the extent of the

161

sickness at the time, or that I would need these things. I wonder if I would be burdening them by making them re-live the events we shared together. It does not seem right. Neither does it seem right to burden my wife or my friends with this garbage.

One thing has me most curious, a trick of human psychology. Why do we all feel inadequate? Why do all the real heroes feel like they are not heroes? I am no hero. Sure, I went to help, but I am no hero. The guy who led the trapped victims out of the darkness with a flashlight is a hero. The people who overpowered the terrorist on United Airlines Flight 93 that went down in Pennsylvania were heroes. The firemen who rushed to help with the evacuation of the burning towers, they are heroes.

I have to tell myself I did my best up there. I did not kill those people.

One thing I can say with honor. My family thinks that I am a hero. As long as they think I am a hero, so be it. I will accept that mantle gladly.

But I wonder about the other side of things, the dark side of this war. There are heroes on the other side. Those terrorists who gave their lives are heroes in their society. They pray to their God and they do what they think is right, even though I do not agree with the indiscriminate taking of a human life. Their government reveres them like our government reveres us. In the streets of these terrorist nations there are banners of fallen men who strapped bombs on their chests and walked into buildings and exploded. Their children want to grow up to be like them. Their mothers are proud and hope that their brothers will do likewise and take up the cause of the jihad.

They use the term martyr, meaning someone who sacrifices their life for their beliefs. But I thought that a martyr was someone who was put to death by the enemy, not someone who took their own life. These are confusing times, but it makes me think.

In the meantime I will do what I do best these days. I will try to heal and I will pray.

Monday
October 8

     I received a curious email today that spells out the statistics. I am sure it has been around through the Internet but in case you haven't seen it, here it is:

** Survival rate **

By now everyone has been hearing the death toll rise and reports of the destruction from the terrorist attacks on the US. These were deplorable acts that we will never forget. But now is a time to look at the other side of the numbers coming out of New York, Washington and Pennsylvania.

The sad but somewhat uplifting side that the mainstream media has not reported yet - the SURVIVAL rates.

*** The Buildings ***

* The World Trade Center -
The twin towers of the World Trade Center were places of employment for some 50,000 people. With the missing list of just over 5,000 people, that means 90% of the people targeted survived the attack. A 90% on a test is an 'A'.

* The Pentagon -

Some 23,000 people were the target of a third plane aimed at the Pentagon. The latest count shows that only 123 lost their lives. That is an amazing 99.5% survival rate. in addition, the plane seems to have come in too low, too early to affect a large portion of the building. On top of that, the section that was hit was the first of five sections to undergo renovations that would help protect the Pentagon from terrorist attacks. It had recently completed straightening and blastproofing, saving untold lives.

This attack was sad, but a statistical failure.

*** The Planes ***

* American Airlines Flight 77

This Boeing 757 that was flown into the outside of the Pentagon could have carried up to 289 people, yet only 64 were aboard. Luckily 78% of the seats were empty.

* American Airlines Flight 11

This Boeing 767 could have had up to 351 people aboard, but only carried 92. Thankfully 74% of the seats were unfilled.

* United Airlines Flight 175

Another Boeing 767 that could have sat 351 people only had 65 people on board. Fortunately it was 81% empty.

* United Airlines Flight 93

This Boeing 757 was one of the most uplifting stories yet. The smallest flight to be hijacked with only 45 people aboard out of a possible 289 had 84% of its capacity unused. Yet these people stood up to the attackers and thwarted a fourth attempted destruction of a national landmark, saving untold numbers of lives in the process.

*** In Summary ***
Out of potentially 74,280 Americans directly targeted by these inept cowards, 93% survived or avoided the attacks. That's a higher survival rate than heart attacks, breast cancer, kidney transplants and liver transplants - all common, survivable illnesses.

The Hijacked planes were mostly empty, the Pentagon was hit at its strongest point, the overwhelming majority of people in the World Trade Center buildings escaped, and a handful of passengers gave the ultimate sacrifice to save even more lives.

Pass this information on to those in fear and the media.

Don't fear these terrorists.

The odds are against them.

When Bin Laden says God - make that a little 'G' and You Got it Right!

It was good to see these statistics and I thank whoever compiled them and sent them out into the world.

Thursday
October 11

It has been one month. The news shows are full of stories about the World Trade Center Disaster. The whole story is told again, the graphic footage of the two planes hitting the towers mixed with pictures of the rescue operations. Then the drama of the collapsing buildings and the eerie scenes of the aftermath where you hear the chorus of screaming alarms, each sounding the location of a downed hero. The darkness of the sky, the rain of ash and the caustic, gagging dust of pulverized concrete in every breath. There is a scene of a fireman sharing his air with a man in a tattered business suit before directing him to safety.

The nightmare is real. I think I am over it but it is real. The dreams are real. What I went through is real. I don't believe it, having seen it with my own eyes and now witnessing these images on television, I don't believe it. Maybe it is because I don't want to believe it, just like the attack on the USS Cole and the bombing of numerous embassies, these events seem too fantastic. I want to go back, back into a world where I don't have to talk Mister Rogers out of committing suicide, where I don't have to see the horror that men can do to each other. We are all God's children. It's hard to remember that, but it is true for Moslems and Christians and Jews and whoever else may be living on this planet. This is the testing ground where the spirit is forged, where we make the decisions that write our lives into the great eternity, the record of how we will be remembered and how we will also remember ourselves.

I still do not understand what entices someone to mail Anthrax or to hide a bomb in a rental truck or to fly a plane full of innocent people into a building. Help me, Greg. You said everyone has a purpose in life. Explain this to me. All I can figure out from this is that it must be some kind of test for America, of what we

167

really stand for. You don't really know if you are going to be a hero in a given situation. Lots of people theorize and project scenarios. We would all like to think of what we would do in an emergency, how we would act and behave. Think of what it must have been like to be one of the firemen or policemen who came upon that scene. If I can't believe it, what must they have thought? Would I stop to think about it or would I run blindly into a burning building in search of trapped and frightened people? I can't really answer that, not unless I was put to the test. Like the scientist who performs experiments on mice, trying to predict which direction they will take in a maze, he never really knows until he performs the experiment and records the results. The results here are amazing, we have a lot of heroes to honor.

We are all heroes to a degree. We all have our battles to fight, our problems to overcome. Is that what's going on here Greg? Have these terrorists just given us the opportunity to prove what we are made of?

I'm raving now, trying to make sense out of a senseless act. It doesn't make the pain any less or take away the grief. I did not kill those people. It's not my fault. I did what I could to help. These are the symptoms of Traumatic Stress Syndrome, Critical Incident Stress Syndrome 2, Post Traumatic Stress Syndrome, and the other names it is called in the pamphlets given to me by Barbara. It is part of Recovery.

Which is what this was all about. The name of the book is Response and Recovery. I am now in recovery. I am healing.

There is nothing more to say.

Except Bonnie raises the big question. "If something happened and FEMA called, would you go again?"

I think about it. It is a different world now, with different disasters. It's not just cleaning up after hurricanes or responding to a flood. There is a new element of danger. I know the answer but I do not want to say it. She looks at me. She knows the answer too. This lab rat is too predictable.

She tells me that I am a hero and I genuinely accept that mantle for once. It puts me in good company.

THE END

August, 2019
Afterwards

Eighteen years have passed. I write this as an afterward, and to add one more piece to this story. In 2002, I started to write a book called *Sword of Fire*. It was finally published in 2016. It is about an angel who takes his young daughter to Earth to show her what angels do. The events of 911 were still strong in my mind when I wrote this, and the following excerpt from that book will give you another perspective on the World Trade Center Disaster.

To set the scene, they emerge from the Firmament that separates Heaven from Earth and find the sky crowded with prayers. In my narrative, the prayers stretch like golden cords from the hearts of the petitioners all the way to the ears of God. I can only imagine what it sounded like that day, and rather than skip right to the action, let me introduce this brief excerpt by including my theories about prayer.

"What is that noise, Father?" she asks.

"It is the sound of prayers," I explain to her.

"But it's so loud," she says, reaching towards her ears.

"We are passing through the medium between that which lies above the Firmament and below. Sound, especially the sound of prayers, is amplified by this medium, much the way water will amplify sounds when we are immersed in it."

"Do all prayers travel this path?" she asks.

"Some bounce right back to Earth and never get this far," I say. "God does not need to hear all prayers. The Firmament acts ealmost like a filter. Prayers with particular vibrations bounce back, such as prayers for world peace, for the health of a loved one, or for light and knowledge. These prayers are amplified and made more powerful. They have a saying on Earth that God helps those who help themselves. This is one way that this power becomes manifest. When the prayers bounce back the high vibration prayers become brighter and stronger. Prayers for health, for example, return to find the loved ones they are intended for, surrounding them with a healing energy. It vitalizes them with the combined power of God's love and prayer."

"How can that be?" she asks.

"God lives in all men's hearts, whether they sense it or not," I explain. "That is the true source of power. When the intention is pure, it causes a perfect reflection, a true image of the purpose of the prayer. The prayer always finds its destination."

"What if, like you said, it is a prayer for world peace?" she asks. "A prayer like that doesn't have a particular destination. What happens when it reflects back towards the Earth?"

"When it hits this filter, it explodes like a star and rains back upon the Earth, scattering like seeds in the wind. Wherever the pieces fall, positive effects are felt."

"So why isn't the Earth all healed and happy?" she asks. "It seems like everyone would be happy if this were the case."

"It would be if everyone wanted world peace," I say. "Don't worry, there will be world peace one day, when men find God in their hearts and offer up more selfless prayers."

"And what about the other prayers?" she asks. "You said other kinds of prayers are bounced back. What are these bouncing prayers?"

"Selfish prayers," I say. "These prayers actually go nowhere. These are low vibration prayers for money, fame, Earthly things. Good people work hard for their dreams and give prayers of thanks, but these selfish prayers are different. They bounce back and fall to Earth, unfulfilled, settling like dust at the feet of the petitioners."

She nods in understanding as I continue. "Sometimes they can come true, but often in horrific ways. For example, a man prays for money, imagining he is getting a large sum. He prays and prays, creating strong thought forms that act to solidify his wishes. One day he cuts his hands off in milling machine, only to find that he is unable to hold the check for the large sum of money that the insurance company sends him as a settlement for the accident. Worse, the money goes not for his imagined luxuries, but for the necessities of his new life."

"Then there are these kinds of prayers, the type we are hearing now, those that penetrate the barrier between Heaven and Earth." I stretch out my free hand and grab the sound wave. The prayer becomes tangible, solidifying like a golden rope in my grasp. "Hold on to me," I say. She squeezes my hand and I grip it tight. "This prayer is a desperate call for help. See how easily it becomes solid?"

"How could you tell it was important?" she asks.

"By its color," I say. "The more urgent the prayer, the brighter it's color."

"What makes these prayers special?" she asks.

173

"I really don't know," I answer. "But somehow they have the power to reach the very ears of God. This one we are holding is something important. When an angel sees or feels a prayer like this, it has to be investigated."

There is a tug from the prayer we are holding, pulling us with a sense of urgency. "Hold on," I say. "The cry has become even stronger. We'll be on Earth soon, riding on a prayer."

"What will we do when we get there?" she asks.

"It will be time to go to work," I say.

We break through the Firmament and into the sky above the Earth. There are many angels emerging from the clouds, all guided by prayers that lead to the hearts of the callers. An airplane thunders below us where they converge. The plane lurches and dips low into the sky, as if to fall, but guided instead with deadly purpose.

"Oh, no," she cries, realizing what I have already seen. The plane is headed towards a building, one of two tall towers of glass standing beside the waters of a great city. I follow the string of the prayer I hold, realizing that she has let go of my hand and found a prayer of her own to follow.

Inside the plane people are crying. A man dark with evil intent faces terrified passengers. A limp body lies in a pool of blood blocking the aisle before him. The same blood stains a box cutter gripped firmly in his right hand. "You may use your cell phones now if you like," he says in a calm voice.

My prayer leads to a woman. Beside her is a small child. She looks at the child, a tear in her eye, but he does not look back at her. He stares out the window. On the wing I see my daughter smiling. The child laughs and she beckons him as if inviting him to play. The woman looks out the window and I think she can see my little

174

angel too. She mutters another prayer to God and I whisper in her ear, "Be not afraid, for I am with you. God has sent an angel to guide you home."

At that moment the plane crashes into the building and fire erupts all about us. Her spirit is jarred loose, knocked free of the flames. She holds her child in her arms, clinging to what she can, but he is already becoming ethereal. His little body is gone, and like a butterfly freed from life as a caterpillar, he suddenly emerges with full wings. So it is with those who die in innocence. The wings spread apart, and now he is holding his mother aloft. I help him by cradling her body in my powerful arms, my daughter beside me. All around us we see angels doing the same, holding beings aloft in their arms.

"It's beautiful," the woman says, as if seeing us for the first time.

"Yes, it is," I reply. I did not want her to look down and see the tragedy unfolding before us. Flames begin to blacken the sky as the tower burns, but I hold her firm. I point out the line of prayer that led us to her. It stretches from her heart to a light in the distant sky, an iridescent rainbow of hope.

"Look, Mommy," says the little boy. "I see God."

"Yes. Now you must go to Him," I say softly. "Hold onto this prayer and it will guide you to Him." The golden cord tugs at her heart, pulling her towards the Firmament above. "Go," I say. "Paradise waits for you. Rest and peace after a lifetime of pain and Earthly suffering."

"Will you be there too?" the little boy asks, turning to my daughter.

"In a little while," she says.

"Will you play with me?" he asks her.

"Of course," she smiles. "But you must hurry. You and your Mom must hurry. Follow your prayers, for they have been answered," she says.

Pride may be a sin, but I could not have been more proud of her at that moment. All regrets I had about bringing her to Earth suddenly disappeared. Celestial work and acts of kindness are what angels do after all.

We watch for a moment as the child and his mother are drawn away from us on gossamer threads, pulled back to the source of all life. Many other souls recede into the distance, pulled by threads that weave in and around each other into a tapestry made from pure love.

We do not have time to enjoy it anymore, for below us a scene of great tragedy unfolds. More angels appear, God's own rescue workers. Around the burning building men and women rush about. Some have angels at their sides, guiding them to unseen places. Others hold back the morass of humanity that rushes forward to help. I quickly lose sight of my daughter, for she has fallen to Earth, speeding towards a group of children who are evacuating a nearby school. Before I can react a second plane appears, flying low and ominous in the sky. Anxious fingers point, and it becomes all too clear what is about to happen. More flames erupt as the airplane plunges into the second tower. Cries and prayers also erupt, a fountain of petitions, blessings, and hopes that bounce off the Firmament and shower down upon the writhing mass of humanity like a torrent of cooling water.

A golden stairway suddenly drops from the shower of prayers, reaching from the clouds to settle gently beside the collapsing pile of rubble. I have seen Jacob's ladder only a few times in my long lifetime and service as an angel, but never like this. The smoke coils about it, but it is transparent, as if floating in another dimension. The rails glow with golden light, and each stair shimmers like the sun reflected in a clear pool. At the base of the stairs, angels stand, reaching out to souls stumbling towards salvation. "This way, please," they say gently, wrapping them in golden cloaks as they step upon the staircase.

"But I was going down the stairs," I hear one say in astonishment. "I was escaping the building. The stairs were going downward!"

"Yes, they were," the angel says softly. "And now they lead up. Up and into the light."

"It's a miracle," the soul cries.

"Yes, it is," says the angel.

I look in another direction and see a procession of evil. For these poor souls the stairs continue to lead down. The fires never stop and Satan's equivalent to Jacob's ladder, if there can be such a thing, leads them deep into the darkness beneath the Earth. The fire that eats the last remnants of the collapsed buildings burns on their flesh. The flames will never go out and they are prodded onward by demons who appear from crevices and shadows within the rubble.

"What are those, Father?" my daughter asks.

"The Fallen Ones," I say.

Upon hearing my voice, a demon turns to look at me. I recognize in his eyes one who I called friend so long ago, long before the separation of Heaven and Hell. Instead of a cloak of white and wings of golden feathers, his skin is scabbous and blotched, his wings dark nubs that have atrophied like unharvested fruit rotting on the vine. I sense both sadness and a sense of purpose in his eyes, a purpose equal to my own.

"Tartaruch," I say, remembering his name.

He sneers at me, continuing to prod his victims with a rusty spear. "Get away," he warns. "I don't have time for your righteous indignation."

"Why do you do it?" I ask.

"It's my job," he says. "I am set over punishments. These Barons of Wall Street knew well what awaited them in the afterlife. They had their chances at humanity, some of them many times over. I'm here to see they get their just rewards." He brandishes his weapon and narrows his eyes. "Now get away before I decide to collect the reward on your hide."

I watch him work, a smile on his lips as he carries out his heinous tasks. I know Lucifer awaits these souls with anxious arms, taking joy in what he keeps from God, souls the Divine has created from the Light of His celestial love. I imagine the perverse pleasure Satan gets from this act and the twisted satisfaction he gains by denying everlasting light to the condemned.

Then there is the torture, the pleasure that the Fallen Ones derive by inflicting endless pain. By doing this, do they escape their own pain? I do not know what goes on in Hell, but I can imagine the suffering. I wonder what becomes of the mote of God that lives on in the hearts of men. Is there hope in Hell or has Satan found a way to mine these jewels for his own enjoyment.

Then I see him, the Devil himself, standing beside the man from the plane who had only recently held a bloodied box cutter in his hands. Lucifer stares at me. He has an awareness that, though not omniscient, is strong and alert. He smiles, nodding to me. His eyes still upon me, he whispers into the man's ear, "This way," pointing downward. "Your reward awaits you, my friend. Ten thousand virgins, their tongues burning with desire for your flesh." His smile widens as the man begins to descend the fiery staircase. He turns back to smile and Satan shimmers, his image shifting. The man stares back, now seeing the devil as he was taught by the priests of his own religion.

Tartaruch steps forward to lead him away. "He's special," rasps Lucifer. "Something about him I like. Take him to my trophy room." They join the procession, demons prodding them on into a gauntlet of pain. Lucifer comes to my side. "Once again we meet upon the battlefield of Earth to reap our spoils."

I am not afraid, and I resist the urge to become his antonym, staying focused upon my own philosophy of neutrality and the Middle Way. "Yes, my old friend," I say softly, meeting not as adversaries in battle, but as true friends. He sees into my heart and knows, like God, what I am thinking. He knows at that moment that I still love him, that true to God's wishes, it is what I feel for him above all. There is no sadness, only love, the love of finding a long lost brother and wanting to welcome him home.

"I don't need your love," he spits.

"I can't help it," I say.

"I know you can't," he replies, his eyes reflecting hatred where I once found love.

"I miss you," I say.

He has no retort for that. I can only imagine what he is thinking, weighing his loss of Heaven against the pain of Hell. There is a commotion behind him and he sneers at me and retreats, turning to shout for his men to grab more souls and pull them unwillingly down into his domain. About me I look at the scene of destruction, seeing rescue workers and bystanders fight for life, unaware that in the same space and time a fight for death is also underway.

Several of the Fallen Ones rush forward, shielding their eyes from the light. Inspired by the presence of their leader, they run towards the golden staircase. Before hostility can begin, I see Michael descend the staircase, his hands wrapped around a flaming sword that glows with power. Souls ascending the staircase quickly scramble to the side rails, making way for the mighty Archangel. Angels near the ground hasten, moving those destined for Heaven's gate quickly toward the staircase. Devils confront them and the angels form a circle of protection around them. My heart sinks as I see the old lines drawn, good and evil squaring off once again for a battle as old as time.

Satan does not waste an instant. Upon seeing Michael, he reaches into the pit and pulls out his own fantastic weapon, something I had not seen before. It is a stout staff, forked at one end, crackling with the same spark as the mythic Sword of Fire. With it he swipes at the defending angels' feet, pushing them aside like broken timbers.

Michael moves quickly now, opening his wings and flying off the staircase. With his Sword thrust forward he directs it between Satan and the angels, catching the fork amid the tines. The Earth shakes with the power, and at that moment, the second tower collapses. Smoke and debris are everywhere. In the center of that mass, as the smoke clears, I see Michael and Lucifer locked in battle. Fire dances off The Sword and lightning strikes in all directions. People flee, instinctively knowing that more than glass and steel are breaking. The very fabric of time is being ripped once again.

My daughter runs behind me, hiding at my back. I sweep her up, carrying her away from all this to a place of safety.

"Why don't you help them, Father?" she asks, and sadness fills me to tears. Before I can answer her, I notice the Ladder becoming unstable. "Quickly," I say to her. "There are souls at stake."

Several angels form a line and protect the retreating spirits of the dead while demons hiss and claw at them. The Earth shakes again as Michael and Lucifer strike at each other with their mighty weapons. Where is God, I wonder, but I know He is in Heaven, tending to His own business, the business of saving souls, welcoming them and warming them with love after a lifetime of unrest and tragedy. The other end of this staircase is just as busy as this end, cluttered with confusion.

Another crack as Lucifer and Michael fight without regard to those around them. The pits of Hell open wider, swallowing pieces of the buildings and more souls of the damned. The ladder becomes choked with traffic. Both the living and the dead cry out in pain but there is no peace to be found here.

My child clings to my robe and I regret bringing her here. "Is it always like this?" she asks, terrified at what she is seeing.

"Not always," I say. "But it is time for us to retreat."

"But I don't want to leave," she says.

"You must," I say. "It is no longer safe for you here."

"But what about them," she says, indicating the souls, both living and dead, struggling to cope with this nightmare.

"They will be all right," I say. "Look!" I point skyward. The air is filled with angels and Heavenly hosts descending from upon high. Willful to the Word of God, the reserves have been called up. The mightiest Archangels fall into line, quickly attacking the demons

that hold unwilling souls in their grasp. Shouts erupt and weapons clang, souls scream and scurry toward the safety of the Ladder.

Demons pour up from the pits, exploding like a geyser of oil from a fresh derrick. They come from everywhere, the debris, the smoke in the air, the cracks in the pavement, even from the hearts of some men.

I take my daughter away from all this, back through the Firmament and upwards into Heaven. As we clear the filter, I see several small children with her, gripped tightly in her hands. As I had rescued her, so had she managed to rescue them.

I look over at her and she is smiling. The images fade and we are back in our garden, freed from the horrors of that day. Her heart glows gently as the beam of light that began this adventure returns to its source.

I have a new, deeper appreciation of the events and the roles we played. Who says we cannot learn from our children?

ACRONYMS USED IN THIS BOOK – If you really want to see a complete list, search the internet using the words "FEMA acronyms".

CD	Compact Disk
DAE	Disaster Assistance Employee
DFO	Disaster Field Office
EMT	Emergency Medical Technician
ESF	Emergency Support Function
FEMA	Federal Emergency Management Agency
FTP	File Transfer Protocol
GIS	Geographical Information Systems
HM	Hazard Mitigation
IA	Individual Assistance
MERS	Mobile Emergency Response Support
NASA	National Aeronautics and Space Administration
NIMDA	A computer virus. Its name comes from spelling "admin" backwards.
PA	Public Assistance
PCB	Polychlorinated Biphenyl, a toxic substance used in electrical transformers
SQL Server	A Microsoft Database product
USAR	Urban Search and Rescue

Made in the USA
Middletown, DE
09 July 2022

68913403R00106